Voices of the Lakes

Shipwrecks and Our Maritime Heritage

Edited by Steve Harrington

Published by the
Great Lakes Diving Council, Inc.
A private, nonprofit organization

In cooperation with
Maritime Press
P.O. Box 759
St. Ignace, MI 49781

ISBN 0-9624629-4-2

**Other Diving Books by
Steve Harrington**

*Divers Guide to Michigan
Divers Guide to Wisconsin
The Best Adventure Yet*

Contents

Preface

Much of the material in this book is derived from a maritime heritage documentary produced by the Great Lakes Diving Council. Interviews were conducted by Ric Mixter and Steve Harrington.

Behind the scenes, Mike Kohut offered continual support and advice. It was his encouragement and confidence that inspired us. It pleases us more than we can express to have Mike as a friend. He has set a standard of honesty, loyalty, and dedication we hope to emulate.

We must also thank Jim Montcalm whose steadfast friendship and behind-the-scenes work kept us enthused and focused.

Throughout the interviews, no effort was made to influence opinions. Instead, we sought out different viewpoints in an attempt to provide an objective treatment of important issues. Only you, the reader, will be able to determine our success.

Introduction

There are a variety of forces affecting sport diving in the Great Lakes region. Some seek regulation to the extent of prohibiting diving on some shipwrecks altogether. Others strive to keep diving totally free.

At the heart of such conflicts are attitudes and activities of sport divers and the place of maritime heritage in our culture.

Unfortunately, these issues are not new and are likely to stay with us for years to come. We have the means available to us, however, to close gaps and work toward common goals. Whether that occurs will depend upon those who are most interested and dedicated to maritime heritage.

This book is a direct result of a concerted effort to expose various viewpoints and help others recognize issues. It is important to remember that many of these viewpoints are opposing, but that is not necessarily a detriment. Through the exchange of diverse ideas and perspectives it is possible to reach beyond individual agendas and attain goals heretofore unimagined.

Not all views on all issues are represented in this book. Instead, we have selected those who are most respected in the diving community and, in some cases, those who represent particularly unique perspectives. Overall, the material presented here should provide the reader with a background not found elsewhere.

Through the exchange of diverse ideas and perspectives it is possible to reach beyond individual agendas and attain goals heretofore unimagined.

Our goal is to enlighten readers and inspire them to form their own opinions and then act responsibly to add their voices to the chorus striving to improve not just diving, but our quality of life. That action requires involvement. It requires speaking out. And it requires risking ridicule and personal attacks from the less informed.

We believe the Great Lakes offer much more than premier sport diving. We also believe that maritime heritage belongs to all of us and, as divers, we may have special responsibilities. Those responsibilities extend beyond shipwrecks. We must consider our effects on the environment and future generations as well.

Do not misunderstand us. We believe divers must enjoy diving. But at the same time, they must recognize that their underwater experiences are unique and with that comes unique responsibilities.

What is at stake? There is much more than the future of sport diving hanging in the balance. We have the opportunity to affect policy in the contexts of water quality and natural and cultural resource management. These policies--how we respond today, next week, and a year from today--may have profound effects on future generations.

We hope you will join us in our quest to preserve not only quality diving, but our quality of life as well.

Both of us have children and in their eyes we see curiosity and thirst for adventure. We hope you will join us in our quest to preserve not only quality diving, but our quality of life as well.

Ric Mixter   **Steve Harrington**

John B. Green
Pioneer Diver

John B. Green began diving in the Great Lakes in 1841. He recorded his exploits and when he was crippled by a diving accident in the 1850s, he turned them into a series of books. The small books were sold by Green on the streets of Boston for $.25 and were his only means of support for the rest of his life.

Today, Green's words live on in reprints of his little books and provide us with a glimpse of the early days of Great Lakes shipwreck diving. Here, excerpts are reprinted to provide readers with an idea of the extreme dangers and hardships faced by those early divers.

It was in the spring of 1841, as I was walking leisurely along the dock in Oswego, that I first saw diving for lost property. Two men were plunging to the bottom of Oswego River for a box of soap and a clock--two articles which had been stolen and thrown into the water.

*   *   *

Elated by this success, I at once conceived the idea of following diving for lost property as a vocation; and during the same season, I recovered large quantities of freight, which had been lost in the harbor and lake about Oswego; the sale of which was so remunerative, that I resolved to follow Submarine Wrecking in the future, as a business.

*   *   *

This armor was constructed of copper and India rubber. That part constructed of copper was to protect the head, and termed the helmet. It was of oval form, quite large in comparison with the head, and had a

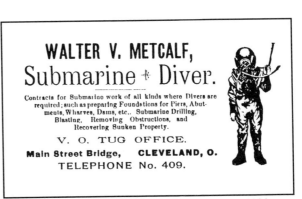

Advertisement from Beeson's Marine Directory, 1884; courtesy Chuck & Jeri Feltner

window in front, and one on each side, for the diver to see through. The rubber covered all the remainder of the body, except the hands, and its dimensions were sufficient to admit an ordinary sized man, with three suits of woolen clothes, which amount was necessary to keep the body warm while underwater. At the top of the helmet was attached the pipe, through which air from the surface, by means of an air-pump, was forced into the armor, keeping it constantly inflated. At the waist of the helmet in front was the escape pipe, for letting off the impure air into the water. There was also in the helmet a valve, which, in case of leakage of the supply pipe, would instantly close and prevent the air from passing out; and another on the end of the escape pipe, which the water would instantly close on rushing into the pipe.

*   *   *

A Frenchman, by the name of M. Klingret, as early as the year 1798, constructed an armor of pieces of tin riveted together in such a way as to make a water-proof encasement for the body. There were two flexible pipes attached to this armor; one which was attached to the head, and terminated in a mouth-piece inside of the armor, and extended to above the surface of the water. When the diver wished to draw a fresh breath, he placed his mouth to the pipe, and took an inspiration.

*   *   *

Another difficulty was the frequent failure of the air to keep the armor so inflated as to prevent the water from compressing the lungs. And I found the whole armor far too light for what it was intended, or at least to dive as deep as even the wreck of the "Erie," much less that of the "Atlantic."

The two armors constructed during this winter were with a view of obviating the difficulty, by attaching the escape pipe at the back part near the top of the head, while the supply pipe was in front, near the pit of the

I had a bag of shot around my neck which weighed about thirty pounds, another around the waist that weighed some ninety pounds, and the shoes weighed about twenty pounds each, making the weight of the armor all together some one hundred and fifty to one hundred and seventy-five pounds.

Even with assistance, pioneer divers needed much strength and endurance. Photo courtesy of Chuck & Jeri Feltner.

stomach, and a heavy breastplate covered the body in front and extended as low as the waist. Added to this I had a bag of shot around my neck which weighed about thirty pounds, another around the waist that weighed some ninety pounds, and the shoes weighed about twenty pounds each, making the weight of the armor all together some one hundred and fifty to one hundred and seventy-five pounds.

I tested this new armor the first opportunity and found it to work far superior to the old one in every respect. It relieved that predisposition to sea-sickness, experienced in the old armor and one could move about under water far more easily.

*　　　*　　　*

I have seen no armor, except those constructed after my improved plan, that will make the diver comfortable while submerged. I have, in a previous chapter, explained the construction of that armor, but I will here recapitulate those points so essential. The air-pipe should be attached at the front near the pit of the stomach, instead of at the top of the helmet; the escape pipe should be at the back of the head, instead of the breast, and it should extend as low as the hips behind. There should be a valve attached at the end of the escape pipe, and also one at the entrance of the air-pipe, that, in case of accident to the air-pipe, the one would prevent the air from escaping, and the other would keep the water from running into the armor while the diver is being drawn to the surface.

*   *   *

When an armor is perfect, the diver can remain down from thirty minutes to nine hours, according to the depth of water; but I am inclined to the opinion that four or five hours is as long as it is prudent to remain under water at a time.

*   *   *

On going to the wreck of the Erie, again, we raised it some fifteen feet, when the cylinder broke away and sunk to the bottom, we again made fast to it, and commenced raising again when the hull broke about forty feet from the bow. We were successful in holding the smaller portion, which we towed to Cattaraugus Creek, where we hoped to find smoother water. When off the harbor at Cattaraugus, I came very near loosing my life, while down to the fragment we had in tow. In some way the signal line, and air pipe became entangled in the purchases lowered to raise the wreck. I could not make my signal understood above. There I was, chained down as it were in some forty feet of water, and to add to my peril it was sun-set and fast growing dark. Death seemed to stare me in the face. But I did not loose the presence of mind which is of all importance to the diver. I put forth every nerve to extricate me from my fettered situation. By great effort I climbed up about six feet, where I cut my signal line, thinking it was clear above, but I found I was mistaken. I made it fast to my wrist, and examined the head-line, (the line by which the diver is drawn up), which I also found entangled, but by cutting it I was enabled to get it free; and I fastened it to my body. I then examined the air-pipe, which I found like the signal line, was entangled in such a manner as to make it impossible to extricate it. To cut this, I knew would be death unless I was instantly drawn up. I again examined the head-line--that I was sure was free. Something I knew must be done at once. I was nearly

Something I knew must be done at once. I was nearly exhausted from toil, in endeavoring to release myself, and the anxiety attending my situation.

exhausted from toil, in endeavoring to release myself, and the anxiety attending my situation. I began to feel sleepy, and with that symptom the diver knows that he must instantly be drawn up.--I was now free except the entanglement of the air-pipe, and I resolved to sever that. I gave signals by means of the signal line, a jerk from which, always was understood to raise. I waited until I was drawn up as far as I could be, at that instant I with one slash, cut the air pipe, and in a moment was on the surface. The reader will at once agree with me, that my effort alone saved me from a watery grave. Had I been so much frightened that I could not work or have sent up the signs of distress to those above in season, I might have lost my life.

> *Had I been so much frightened that I could not work or have sent up the signs of distress to those above in season, I might have lost my life.*

*   *   *

I then arose for a rope and hook, and found that I had been down just forty-seven minutes, but, notwithstanding, felt perfectly well, and would have instantly returned had the rope and hook been at hand. As they were not, I removed the face of the armor, and sat down to wait for the implements. I had sat but a moment, when a sharp pain shot like lightning through my lower extremities, and the next instant it went through my whole system, so prostrating me that I could not move a limb, or even a muscle. I was immediately taken to Port Dover, where I had medical attendance procured me. After lying here two weeks, I was brought to Buffalo, where I received every attention. The best physicians pronounced me incurable. I remained in Buffalo ten days, but I did not improve in the least. I was then removed to my home in

Boston, where it was five tedious months before I could step; and in the spring I was only so far recovered as to walk a very little with crutches.

*   *   *

In diving on the outside of Middle Island, in Lake Huron, I frequently found places where the water was rushing down through the rocky bottom at the slope of the reef. I descended into these crevices a short distance, but as this was after I was paralyzed, I feared I might be drawn into some small crevice by the force of the current as I had not my usual strength in my crippled state.

*   *   *

One great requisite to success in diving is endurance, to which must be added cool judgment, perseverance, and a determination to go through thick and thin, and not cower.... Without the above requisites, no person need think of becoming a diver; for the pain which he will have to endure in deep water will make any but a stubborn heart retreat.

What improvements may hereafter be made in diving I will not pretend to say; yet, I am convinced that there can be much progress in the art. Still, it has already been brought to such perfection that it imparts to commerce a valuable practical benefit; while by the aid of sub-marine armor, the bodies of friends and relatives may be rescued from their watery graves, and deposited where their last resting places may be known.

One great requisite to success in diving is endurance, to which must be added cool judgment, perseverance, and a determination to go through thick and thin, and not cower.... Without the above requisites, no person need think of becoming a diver; for the pain which he will have to endure in deep water will make any but a stubborn heart retreat.

Mike Kohut
Sport Diver/Retailer

Mike Kohut, with his wife, Linda, founded Recreational Diving Systems, Inc., in Royal Oak, Michigan. Together, they built one of the largest dive centers in the Midwest, but more than that, they contribute immensely to Great Lakes sport diving. Mike's involvement includes helping draft legislation and consulting on training and equipment design. He is a former president of the Michigan Underwater Preserve Council and is the current president of the Straits of Mackinac Underwater Preserve Committee. He is an international expert on sport diving and dive travel.

Although retired, Mike continues to monitor Great Lakes sport diving developments. He is a valued supporter of the Great Lakes Diving Council.

Who are sport divers?

Sport divers include the whole range of the general population from children as young as 12 years old to people in their late 60s and 70s. There are some very active sport divers in their 80s.

Why do people dive?

People usually dive for two different reasons. One is negative thrill. That is when someone feels they are cheating death by going underwater. The other reason people dive is for the simple enjoyment of the freedom and relaxation offered by the underwater environment.

People who get into diving from a negative thrill perspective are ones who often end up diving for less than a year. They find themselves on dive boats with women, children and people in their 60s and 70s. They realize that scuba diving really isn't that dangerous. These people go down after one or two dives and find they are extremely comfortable and they realize that scuba diving is not cheating death. Sometimes they go on to some other sport such as sky diving.

The people who are into it from a relaxation standpoint enjoy the underwater environment because there are no telephones and they can

17

totally relax. These people discover they can cruise in a weightless environment. It is an experience they can't find elsewhere.

If scuba diving is not that dangerous, then why is there a general perception of danger?

Diving is not dangerous but diving has inherent risks. We are underwater. We are in an alien environment and we can not breathe water.

We can take what we need to survive--air--down with us. The air supplies will last anywhere from a half-hour to an hour and a half depending on the size of the tank and the breathing rate of individuals.

> *Diving is not dangerous but diving has inherent risks.*

The risk arises when a diver is not comfortable underwater. When a person is in a stress situation the first reaction is to escape from the stress. Normally, underwater, the escape route is straight up and that is the biggest risk--coming up too fast.

As long as the diver is relaxed and has the ability to think, the risk is minimized. Divers must remember to keep their heads and remember that if they need to come up for any reason they can do so with a slow, controlled ascent.

Have equipment improvements made diving safer?

Yes, major equipment improvements have made diving both safer and easier.

Regulators deliver air almost as easily as breathing on the surface so with a good quality regulator, divers will never get into a situation where they will feel starved for air. Today's quality regulators provide air at a rate and in a manner that avoids concerns about divers receiving sufficient air.

> *Equipment improvements have made diving both safer and easier.*

The other big safety device that has been developed in recent years is the buoyancy compensator. These compensators allow divers to relax and float at the surface without any effort. Divers can come up away from the boat or away from shore. All they have to do is inflate the buoyancy compensator and just simply relax and swim in at a slow leisurely rate. The buoyancy compensator has removed the panic involved with swimming distances. Now, there is no big rush or panic.

Has scuba diving become a true family activity or is this an activity still restricted to adults?

It has definitely become a family activity.

The minimum age to learn to dive is 12 years old and if there are children diving they really should be under the direct supervision of an adult at all times. Scuba diving should not be thought of as an activity where an adult would take two, three, or four children between the ages of 12 and 14 and just send them off diving on their own. There is some judgment required as far as where to go, when to go, and types of dives to make. Many times, young children have not yet attained the maturity they need to make those types of judgments.

Young divers can even feel too comfortable underwater and will either lose sight of the risk or perhaps not understand it from the beginning. We always recommend for young children that they dive under the direct supervision of a parent or adult.

Do we need additional government involvement in Great Lakes sport diving?

We don't we need any government intervention in diving. The diving itself has been self-policed by the diving community. We have different organizations that oversee the certification standards for divers and instructors. If we look at diving safety statistics we see it has become a much

Diving has become a family activity.

safer sport than it was even just 20 years ago. The number of injuries and accidents is way down in total numbers and at the same time the number of divers is way up. So we are seeing an increase in the number of people participating and an actual decrease in the number of accidents.

Government involvement would have no effect on diving safety and would only drive up the cost of diving.

That is a very fine safety record and is a strong argument against government involvement. Government involvement would have no effect on diving safety and would only drive up the cost of diving.

What about government intervention to protect resources...or can divers police themselves?

Yes, divers can police themselves. If we are considering government intervention strictly as a means of protecting the resources, we have laws on the books now for that purpose. We find that divers are really the only ones who are going to be able to enforce those laws by controlling their own behavior and reporting violators.

We are never going to be able to have any type of dive police under any jurisdiction on all the wrecks all of the time. So if someone wants to destroy a resource, whatever it might be--a reef in the Caribbean or a shipwreck here--they are going to be able to do that at some point no matter what the government does or how many police we have.

We really must educate divers about the value of shipwreck conservation. And to a great extent, the diving community has done an excellent job in that regard. We are seeing more and more divers in the Great Lakes area who really care about the resources.

Our shipwrecks have remained in good condition primarily because we have made the case that these are important recreational resources. We have not emphasized the historic values because those values are sometimes difficult to express or appreciate.

We are finding that divers do not want to destroy their own recreational resources.

Instead, we have focused on the excitement of diving shipwrecks with many artifacts still at the site. We are finding that divers do not want to destroy

20

A diver explores the Murray Bay wreck at the Alger Underwater Preserve near Munising, Michigan. Photo by Mike Kohut.

their own recreational resources.

We find the same approach in the ocean with coral reefs. Divers are not down there purposely destroying reefs. We have seen a huge shift with training in buoyancy control and in keeping divers off the reef so they do not break off coral accidentally. With the very rare exception, divers are very happy to do what they can to protect these kinds of recreational resources.

Have you seen a major shift in diver ethics then?

In the past we had many divers collecting artifacts not with the intent to steal but to show friends and family what diving is like. They wanted to share with others the excitement they felt while diving and artifacts was one way to do that.

What we are seeing now, with the advent of good and inexpensive underwater photography and video equipment, is that it is much easier and rewarding for divers to share through images. Divers have discovered they no longer have to remove artifacts to share their sport. Now, they can see it on video or in photographs and derive as much--if not more--satisfaction from that type of sharing.

Michigan's underwater preserves appear very successful. How do you see their role in fostering a conservation ethic among divers?

Underwater preserves were probably not required to protect underwater resources. There were concentrations of shipwrecks in certain areas and the original notion was that preserves could offer some protection.

What happened is that the underwater preserve attracted more divers to those areas. And with more and more divers we found increasing interest in protecting those resources. The ethic actually grew from the use and appreciation of the resources.

It is important to recognize that conservation really started with the divers who learned about the resources and appreciated them and not necessarily the state.

> **The ethic actually grew from the use and appreciation of the resources.**

We went from two preserves in 1980 to nine with two more pending designation. The laws protecting shipwrecks and other submerged resources are virtually identical to the protection laws outside the preserves. But the value of underwater preserves is the designation of an area as having a concentration of shipwrecks and other submerged attractions. Divers know they can find attractions in these areas and they also know there are services that facilitate diving.

In this way, underwater preserves have done a great job of focusing attention on the resources and promoting diving. Actual protection of the resources is probably a secondary function of the preserves.

A marine sanctuary has been proposed by the National Oceanic and Atmospheric Administration (NOAA) for Thunder Bay in Lake Huron. Do you believe we need a marine sanctuary in the Great Lakes?

They are considering most of Thunder Bay as a marine sanctuary, which would be administered by the federal government.

Many people believe that if the area becomes a marine sanctuary the federal government will throw tons of money at that area. Some local business people believe designation will bring a plethora of cash for them. I think they will be a little surprised if designation actually occurs.

As far as protection of the resources is concerned we will probably find no more real protection of resources under a marine sanctuary than we will under the current underwater preserve system.

We will probably find that once a marine sanctuary is designated there are many more restrictions on diving and other water-related activities. That could hurt Great Lakes diving in the long run. People could be easily intimidated by or resentful of the additional layer of government and simply avoid the area. They will simply go to other areas where it is easier to recreate.

In the end, it is possible that NOAA marine sanctuary designation will actually reduce diving in the area instead of promoting diving. Local business people could be very surprised to find fewer tourism dollars as a result.

We could also find that a marine sanctuary could have a devastating effect on other Great Lakes resources because one of the findings required for a NOAA marine sanctuary is that the state is incapable of managing its own resources. That could jeopardize Michigan's other preserves. Designation could raise many issues about the current law.

> *I doubt that designation would bring the tourists and cash local business people hope it will.*

I doubt that designation would bring the tourists and cash local business people hope it will. Like anything new, there could be a sudden increase in the number of visitors but that boom, if there is one, would be short-lived.

What is it about Michigan diving that is so appealing?

The Great Lakes offer some of the finest shipwreck diving in the world because of the fact that once the ships go down in the Great Lakes they are so well preserved. We don't have the wood worms and such that eat and deteriorate the wood on shipwrecks. We don't have the salt and corrosion that eat the steel and iron on ships so our shipwrecks are well-preserved.

A diver can go down on a ship that went down 100 or 150 years ago and the wood is still intact. The wood may absorb water and soften a little bit but you can actually see ships as you think ships look like. They appear not as scattered pieces on the bottom but as intact vessels. In some cases, the paint can still be found on wooden schooners that went down more than a century ago.

As a result, we have some of the finest shipwreck diving in the Great Lakes. Our collection of shipwrecks is the very best in the world.

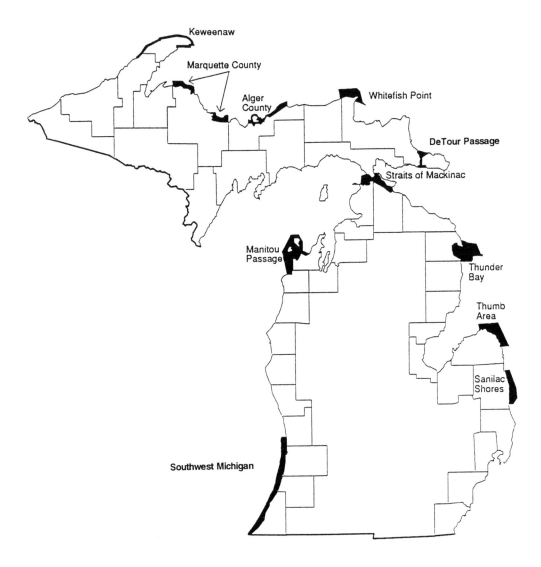

Keweenaw

Marquette County

Alger
County

Whitefish Point

DeTour Passage

Straits of Mackinac

Manitou
Passage

Thunder
Bay

Thumb
Area

Sanilac
Shores

Southwest Michigan

Michigan's Underwater
Preserve System

Do you have a favorite of all the preserves?

My favorite area is the Straits of Mackinac Underwater Preserve. The Straits area doesn't offer the clearest water of the preserves, but it offers protection from weather. There is almost no day that you can't get out somewhere on one of the wrecks to dive.

The area also offers a large variety of shipwrecks. We have shipwrecks that run from a 600-foot modern steel freighter just like you see sailing on the lakes today to old schooners that sank in the 1850s. The shipwrecks in the Straits area tend to be more intact.

They are generally upright and easy to dive. On one weekend in the Straits you can dive on a steel freighter, old wooden schooners, or wooden steamers from the 1800s. And the local community has developed several shore-access sites near St. Ignace so it is easy to dive the Straits of Mackinac Underwater Preserve even if you do not have access to a boat.

What do you see for sport diving in the future?

From here I don't think we're going to see a lot of changes. We're seeing some deterioration of the wrecks through natural processes such

A diver examines the wreckage of the C.H. Johnson in the Straits of Mackinac Underwater Preserve. Photo by Mike Spears.

as waves and ice. The biggest changes may come with the spread of zebra mussel infestations.

So far, zebra mussel colonies have been limited to the lower Great Lakes but it is possible that they will spread north. It may be a function of available nutrients and water temperature.

The problem with zebra mussels is that their colonies obscure shipwreck features. But they also filter the water and can greatly increase visibility. We've seen visibility in Lake Erie, which was long considered a dead lake, go from zero to as much as 40 or 50 feet. That is a direct result of zebra mussels.

The unfortunate part is that even though we can see 40 or 50 feet all we can really see are the zebra mussels. Zebra mussels sometimes form colonies eight inches thick. For this reason the biggest threat to Great Lakes shipwreck diving is the zebra mussel.

What about the cold water of the Great Lakes? What effect will this have on diving?

The cold water and restricted visibility are probably the two biggest detriments to Great Lakes diving. The cold water can be overcome with good wetsuits and drysuits. Beyond that, we have probably gone as far as we can with passive insulation in a wetsuit or a drysuit.

We are going to find ways to heat the diver so the diver will be able to explore deeper depths and not just survive but actually enjoy a fair measure of comfort.

The next generation of exposure protection will bring active heating--either chemically or electrically. We are going to find ways to heat the diver so the diver will be able to explore deeper depths and not just survive but actually enjoy a fair measure of comfort.

What incentive is there for divers to go from warm water diving, such as the Caribbean, to Great Lakes diving?

Perhaps the most compelling reason to dive the Great Lakes is the shipwrecks. Divers are able to enjoy shipwrecks and similar attractions in the Great Lakes and only in the Great Lakes.

Another reason for diving the Great Lakes is convenience. The Great Lakes are accessible to large numbers of divers every weekend. Many divers are making Great Lakes diving an after-work activity.

The Alger Underwater Preserve is in the process of intentionally sinking a tugboat as a diving attraction. Is this important to Great Lakes diving?

The biggest advantage that intentionally sinking a new shipwreck is that you can choose where you want to sink it. It can be sunk in a sheltered area and in a manner that makes it accessible for most divers. Also, it can be sunk at a favored depth. It can be located in a place that is deep enough to avoid navigation problems but shallow enough for most divers.

Intentional sinking of old ships is nothing new. It has been done all up and down the Atlantic and Pacific coasts, primarily as artificial reefs and a lot of it was done for sport fishing; at least that was the original intent.

The 71-foot tugboat, the Steven M. Selvick, is scheduled to become the first intentionally sunken vessel for U.S. sport divers. Photo by jim Montcalm.

Now we're finding ships that are being sunk just as dive sites. The Coast Guard cutters *Duane* and *Bibb* in the Florida Keys are excellent examples. Those two ships were sunk in the 1980s and in a few short years have become the most popular dive sites in the Keys.

There is an attraction to shipwrecks for divers and intentional sinking can also make diving more attractive and safer. The ships can be sunk in a manner that ensures they remain upright on the bottom and before the sinking, hatches and doors can be removed or welded open for safety.

Will intentional vessel sinking mean a big boom in Great Lakes shipwreck diving?

There will always be a short-term boom and a taper off. That's true of anything new, but there will be long-term benefits as well. Statistics show that divers tend to dive on ships whether they've been artificially placed or are the result of natural disasters.

There's a tendency for some people to say divers aren't going to go down there because they know it was intentionally sunk. But statistically that's not true. People enjoy exploring the ships. They enjoy looking around and seeing first hand how vessels were constructed and operated. Intentionally sunk or otherwise, this is part of our maritime heritage.

Charles E. Feltner
Maritime Historian/Diver

Charles "Chuck" Feltner, and his wife Jeri, made their first Great Lakes shipwreck dives in the Straits of Mackinac in 1977. Since that time, their names have become synonymous with many of Michigan's best-known shipwrecks.

Chuck and Jeri have discovered, explored, documented, and written about many of the most important and most visited shipwrecks in the state. More than that, Chuck and Jeri are wonderfully intelligent, articulate, and caring people who epitomize the best of Great Lakes divers. Their teamwork has led to the discovery of many popular shipwrecks, including the *Sandusky* and *Northwest*.

Chuck and Jeri have contributed immensely to our body of knowledge of Great Lakes maritime history through their painstaking research and excellent writing. Here, Chuck shares his thoughts about Great Lakes shipwreck diving: past, present, and future.

In order to look at the future of Great Lakes diving--to know where it is headed--we must also understand where it has been. It is as though there are two Great Lakes diving frontiers--the old and the new--and we must first examine the old frontier to understand the new.

Jeri and I started diving in the early 1970s and at that time there was a great deal of adventure in the sport. There was a great sense of exploration and discovery because so much of the Great Lakes was unexplored territory. Shipwreck hunting, in particular, wasn't something widely pursued. It also wasn't widely accessible to everyday people.

During this time, Great Lakes diving saw much growth. There were many divers who had an adventurous nature and became involved in wreck searching. And along with this there came the evolution of hero figures--pioneers who other people sought to emulate. These people are the likes of Dick Race, Dave Trotter, and John Steel. These are people who broke new ground and really began exploring Great Lakes diving. In the process, they opened new vistas for many people.

The question follows, then, where are the new John Steels, Dick Races, and Dave Trotters? I don't see many of them coming along and when they do, it will be in a whole new arena.

What has transpired in Great Lakes shipwreck finding is much like our space program. When our space program was new, we had a whole new frontier ripe for exploration. But, now, we need to ask, where are the new Neil Armstrongs, John Glenns, and Alan Shepards?

Just as there was a frontier with the opening of space, that era, like the era of shipwreck discovery, has largely passed. The adventure is mostly gone because the frontier has been settled. Consider, for example, how many people know the names of the astronauts on the last space shuttle? It has become a ho-hum event.

This is very similar to Great Lakes shipwreck discovery. Finding a new shipwreck today has become a ho-hum event because it is much more common place. Those who search for shipwrecks are much better organized and they have the benefits of new technology. Just as important is the fact that the way has been shown. All that is left is for them to follow in the footsteps of others who have gone before. The challenge will never be the same, regardless of the number of shipwrecks they discover.

All that is left is for them to follow in the footsteps of others who have gone before. The challenge will never be the same, regardless of the number of shipwrecks they discover.

Where are we today? We are at a place where many in diving have settled into a routine and we have no real modern-day heroes. And we need heroes, we need people who accept challenges and lead us on new paths.

Currently, there is much debate about underwater parks registration, and "routinization". That is where the new frontiers will be in diving--making Great Lakes diving accessible to more people. The challenge will be to make diving easier, more accessible, and enjoyable for more people. Special emphasis should be placed on enjoyment--

Special emphasis should be placed on enjoyment-- diving must be enjoyable for the less hearty, less creative, less adventurous, and more common person.

diving must be enjoyable for the less hearty, less creative, less adventurous, and more common person.

The challenge will be to create that kind of inviting environment for divers. That will center largely around shipwreck but also includes other attractions, such as underwater geologic formations.

In the new frontier, the explorers and leaders will emerge and that is already beginning to occur. But serious questions remain whether that frontier will be successfully explored and settled. There must be an economic driver for businesses because business will play an important role in bringing about this exploration and settling.

"Diving must be enjoyable for the less hearty, less creative, less adventurous."
Photo by Steve Harrington

There must be a high enjoyment aspect for the everyday man. We need only to look at tennis to gain an understanding of the dynamics of recreation.

The number of people playing tennis today is about half of what it was in 1980. There has been a substantial decline in only 15 years and the same is true for other sports activities. Today, there are many opportunities for people to spend their time and money for recreation. This is an increasingly busy world with more competition for diving dollars and time.

There is a very great risk that people will not put their time and money into Great Lakes diving. Clearly, that will not happen unless there is an enjoyable environment and that must be brought about by significant leadership.

The Tobermories of the world is where that future is. That is a highly organized situation where people can go and enjoy diving. It is not just the patrol of shipwrecks and dive boats, but also the surrounding, terrestrial

The Tobermories of the world is where that future is.

31

environment. There is an information office where visitors can obtain knowledge about local resources. Also important are the campgrounds, motels, and a "scene" where divers can meet other divers and enjoy the social aspects of the sport. It is this supporting environment on land that may mean much to the eventual success or failure of this frontier.

Will the necessary leadership be there? Will the economic incentives be there? These are questions that must be asked and the answers will likely determine the future of Great Lakes sport diving.

There is also the ancillary question as to whether the maritime research needed for this new frontier will exist. Extensive maritime research was required for the old frontier and it was needed at a time when there were no formal maritime research methods and difficult access to resources.

There was a great deal of confusion in maritime research when I started. The only sources of information were the information hoarders who used the information as a power base. That's largely been broken open and now we're beginning to see significant programs that make this information easier to access. It is becoming more user friendly. Good examples are found at the Milwaukee Public Library and the Kingston museum where information is readily available to people of all walks of life.

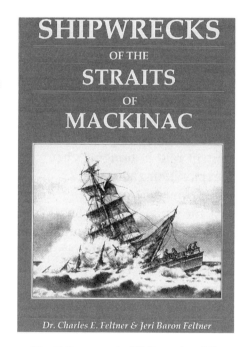

SHIPWRECKS
OF THE
STRAITS
OF
MACKINAC

Dr. Charles E. Feltner & Jeri Baron Feltner

The Feltners wrote "Shipwrecks of the Straits of Mackinac," the most comprehensive work on this topic to date.

It remains to be seen whether leadership will emerge and cooperation among various maritime heritage organizations becomes commonplace. There is much potential in such organizations as the Association for Great Lakes Maritime Heritage.

Working together, Great Lakes diving may lead to these new frontiers that are based on inclusion of many people rather than the very exclusive frontier of the past.

Frank Cantelas
Maritime Archaeologist
East Carolina University

Frank Cantelas is a staff maritime archaeologist with East Carolina University in Greenville, North Carolina. He led two seasons of field archaeological work at the site of a 65-foot schooner believed to have been wrecked near Naubinway, Michigan in the 1840s. He took time from his work to explain archaeological techniques and findings. He was interviewed by Nick Burnett and Ric Mixter during field work at the Naubinway site.

How long is the cargo hold?

It's about 25 feet long inside the ship. You can see the barrels sticking out of the walls so one can get an idea of about how wide it is.

The cargo hold was packed with barrels and the cargo was packed in the barrels. The barrels are built with wooden staves. There are about 16 staves to each barrel and you can see the wooden hoops that secured the barrels. The ends are called heads, or butts, and we have found many markings on the heads.

Why is that important?

The markings include names. These are inspector's names--people who looked at the barrels and the contents to make sure the contents corresponded to labels. It was a pretty common trading practice.

What else have you found?

That is called the mast step and that notch is where the mast actually set down on the keelson of the ship. There was a big square tenet on the bottom of the circular mast and it fit into the notch. The mast would rise up through the deck.

By splashing this timber with water we can get a better look at the keelson. The keelson ran down the center of the ship. It is set in place with iron fasteners and tightened up with a shim.

How were other parts of the ship constructed?

Above us were the ceiling planks and then, under that, you have the ribs or frames of the ship. The frames of the ship are sandwiched between the keelson and the keel, which is on the bottom of the ship.

How long has the ship been here?

The ship probably beached or wrecked about 1840 or so. It's been here about 150 years and nobody has seen it since about 1849. A surveyor saw it in 1849. A government surveyor was mapping the lake shoreline and he mentioned in a report that there was a derelict shipwreck on the beach. At that time, the masts were still on it and he mentioned that.

What is the name of this ship?

We don't know. It doesn't have a name on it. We haven't been able to identify it yet but we're looking into newspaper accounts around 1840 to see what type of ships wrecked in this area. Maybe we'll be able to identify it by looking at newspapers so we're still searching.

What are you doing with all the old barrels?

We've found about 25 different barrels and we've found about four different kinds. What we do is sample the barrels. We identify a particular type and keep about two examples of each type. The rest we excavate. We photograph and measure them and draw them. Then we package them up and when we're done we'll set them into the bottom of the ship and rebury them. That way we don't have to incur the cost of conservation. We don't have to spend time conserving the individual wooden pieces, which takes a considerable amount of time, effort, expense, and supplies.

Are all the barrels broken up?

These barrels seem to have 16 staves. You can see how the edges are beveled. The staves are built in a circle so each one of these barrel staves has to be beveled to fit together to form a circle. You can see

Frank Cantelas shows Nick Burnett the archaeological excavation at Naubinway. Photo by Jim Montcalm

how they are bowed. That creates tension to help seal the barrel seams. And there are two ends to each barrel. The ends are called heads or butts and they are circular pieces of wood. They fit into what is called a crow's screw.

Most of these barrels are about 25 inches tall. They are pretty uniform in size although there is some variability. You can see where there are stained marks on the outside. That is where the bands went around. They used wooden bands in the form of flexible saplings, to hold the hoops or staves in place.

Metal was expensive so they generally used saplings. Saplings were split in half so there was a flat side to put around the barrel staves. The saplings would be notched so they would lock on themselves.

What value is there in burying these barrels and then uncovering them again in the future?

We take a sample of the material so we don't need to recover all of it because we have a good idea of what's going on with just a sample. If there is some question about these barrels I want to ask or, perhaps you would want to ask 20 years in the future, the barrels will be here, well-preserved for that purpose.

Whenever possible, we like to save material for the future. That is because there are always different ways to study archaeology. Each person has their own questions to ask and new technology may be developed to help answer those questions.

What do you know about this ship?

We believe this was a coasting schooner that worked the Great Lakes. It had two masts and probably hauled salted fish from up here and transported it to the lower lakes. On the way back, it would probably haul various supplies to fishing camps.

This wreck was apparently blown ashore and then covered with sand. What advantages do you have working on a vessel in this condition?

Frank Cantelas, left, explains to Nick Burnett about barrel construction and what was found after more than 150 years buried in sand.
Photo by Jim Montcalm.

This vessel is such an intact craft and our techniques are more refined because it is above water. We will be able to obtain more data in a shorter amount of time.

Two years ago, we excavated personal belongings, ship equipment, tools, what was used in their daily life, portions of the cargo and layers of fish bone, and scales. Most surprising this year is the discovery of markings on barrels with individual inspector's names. And there is information regarding the place where the barrels came from. This will give us an indication of when cargo went on board and help us narrow down the date of the vessel's loss. In our previous work, we found the interior of the ship intact. The cabins were still in very good shape. These factors are important in locating clues that can be pieced together later.

David Cooper
Maritime Archaeologist
Wisconsin Historical Society

David Cooper is the maritime archaeologist for the State Historical Society of Wisconsin. Mr. Cooper has been involved in many Great Lakes shipwreck documentations and excavations. He is well-known throughout the Great Lakes region as a leader in shipwreck conservation. It is important to note that Mr. Cooper makes extensive use of trained, volunteer divers in his work.

The most important thing to remember about the study of maritime history on the Great Lakes is that it's really a study of who we are. It is a study of where we came from as a region, as communities, and as individuals.

The Great Lakes were a great natural highway into the interior of the United States and it's no coincidence that these were the first areas explored by European Americans--by the French fur traders in particular--as early as the 1600s.

Green Bay is one of the oldest cities in the United States and that's because of the maritime transportation corridor offered by the Great Lakes. Transportation into this "new world" was so important control became the focus of the whole fight for the northwest frontier during the Revolutionary War and before that the French and Indian War and later the War of 1812. All of that was for control of this great highway into the interior.

It is a study of where we came from as a region, as communities, and as individuals.

The history of the United States in the 19th Century, especially the economic and social development of this area, was due to the Great Lakes and the availability of the water transportation corridor. This was before railroads were built across the country. Sail and then steam power were the most efficient way of moving passengers and freight.

The Great Lakes region was an area of vast natural resources such as timber, coal, salt, furs, and after the timbering there was arable farmland for grain production. The area become a sort of breadbasket of the United States. All of these factors hastened the development of the Great Lakes region and then there was the discovery of iron and copper ore.

These were the natural resources that were heavily exploited on the Great Lakes. The transportation offered by the Great Lakes waterway allowed those areas to be exploited and, in turn, allowed the communities to develop around the Great Lakes. Our major towns began as ports. Look at your Chicago, Milwaukee, Detroit, Cleveland, Duluth, Buffalo; these are all port cities.

Consider the Mississippi River to the west which connects us to the southern states and the Gulf Coast. It is easy to see that the Great Lakes are at the hub of this transportation network coming from the east and from the south. The stories of the ships that sailed these waters, the people who sailed these waters, and the immigrants who were brought into the interior of the United States through these waterways is the history of the Great Lakes.

> *The transportation offered by the Great Lakes waterway allowed those areas to be exploited and, in turn, allowed the communities to develop around the Great Lakes.*

Also important is the freshwater environment we have. It's often called an inland sea but it's not a marine environment--it's a freshwater environment, which is very different ecologically.

It also required a very different type of vessel. Great Lakes ships evolved for navigation in these waters. The Millicoquins wreck, for example, is an important missing link between salt water vessel designs of the Colonial Period and the Medieval Period in Europe. Europeans adapted those vessel designs to a new environment, in this case the inland waterways of the Great Lakes. The only models the Europeans had to base their designs on for a Great Lakes vessel were vessels that sailed the Baltic Sea, the Chesapeake Bay, and the shallow waterways of the East Coast and the Old World.

What we see is a lot of designs from Scandinavia, Germany, England and the East Coast of the United States--New England and the Chesapeake Bay region--brought into the Great Lakes. There were also some adaptions from native designs. Native American watercraft designs were borrowed by the French. The French basically borrowed the birch bark canoe design intact from the Native Americans and just

Small schooners, such as the "Moonlight", were important predecessors to contemporary Great Lakes freighters.

simply enlarged it for commercial haulage up to 10 meters (33 feet).

Those were two separate types of designs. The bateaux and the canoe are smaller craft and were particularly used in the early period of the fur trade during exploration. The schooner designs were the next-larger class of vessels and those were used in the late period of the fur trade. They were also used during the early exploration of the lakes and for early settlements such as fishing camps and general trading.

The early, small schooner is the type of design that would have followed the canoes and the bateaux.

Small schooners were important in the evolution of Great Lakes shipping and as early as the 18th Century the British realized that the schooner and the sloop were the ideal rigs for sailing these waters. The early schooners and sloops were both aft-rigged they had sort of triangular sails that are so familiar on modern sailboats. Those designs are much handier in confined waters like the Great Lakes where there are variable winds.

Another important advantage is that they could be handled with a smaller crew. That's critical on the frontier where manpower is in short supply and money is scarce. Hiring extra personnel can be difficult or uneconomical.

Also the sails could be taken in more quickly on a fore and aft-rigged vessel so they could respond much better to the variable weather of the Great Lakes. Brigs were a square-rigged vessel and were less

> **Small schooners were important in the evolution of Great Lakes shipping.**

efficient in this region.

So, why do we appreciate maritime history? It is because we are looking at the roots of our modern day communities; our modern day Great Lakes. Every one of us, almost regardless of heritage, is touched by Great Lakes maritime heritage. It's a study of ourselves and it starts with something like looking at the physical evidence of the people who preceded us here. In this case, shipwrecks. And the study of certain shipwrecks will help us fill in missing information about how the evolution of Great Lakes shipping occurred.

> *Every one of us, almost regardless of heritage, is touched by Great Lakes maritime heritage.*

It's particularly important for young people now to understand where they came from. The country is becoming increasingly homogenized. We're losing our sense of regionalism. The South is becoming more like the North, the East is becoming more like the West and we're all getting to be very much the average middle Americans. That's good for creating a unified country. Lord knows that the Civil War taught us what sectionalism can do, but it is important for people to understand their roots.

For youngsters, a lot of the reason why youth have problems with identity is this very homogenization. They don't understand what their communities are. It is hard to respect the community if you don't know much about it and it's hard to respect your family unless you understand that heritage.

History has always served an important function in providing us with a sense of self and a sense of our past. It is often said that we don't know where we're going if we don't know where we came from. The important thing to realize is that history is context. It's the context of who we are. And youngsters need that. It is important for youngsters and that's why we teach state history to third and fourth graders. We help them understand early that everyone is part of the historical process that builds communities.

> *History has always served an important function in providing us with a sense of self and a sense of our past.*

There has been a lot of interest in maritime archaeology on the Great Lakes. People are interested in these fantastic excavations but unless you dive it's very difficult to see these sites.

C. Patrick Labadie
Director
Canal Park Museum

C. Patrick Labadie is director of the Canal Park Maritime Museum in Duluth, Minnesota. The museum is operated by the U.S. Army Corps of Engineers.

Pat is well-known in the Great Lakes region as a maritime historian and has a special interest in ship construction and historic photographs of commercial vessels. He is known for his objective views and thoughtful insights on maritime issues.

How do you view divers and their opportunity to practice conservation with shipwrecks?

We seldom find a historical site or shipwreck that isn't already badly disturbed or compromised. I think back not too many years ago when even the shallower, more accessible sites were not so badly disturbed and there were a lot of artifacts. It's a real crime that so many of the artifacts have been removed and the wrecks have been so degraded and so significantly changed.

Not only does this affect the modern diver who can no longer enjoy this same level of experience, but for the rest of us in the academic community who would like to study and make some conclusions about the wrecks. It is no longer possible.

When a diver does have that really rare opportunity to explore a wreck that has some integrity about it, there really is a responsibility to the rest of society to leave them undisturbed.

I'm one of the museum community as well as a diver and I am always torn by some of the issues related to the removal of artifacts. Divers have frequently brought up artifacts and given them to museums and museums have even gone so far as to encourage or sponsor removal of artifacts. This has to be done really really carefully.

It might be a service to the larger public to preserve those artifacts where they can no longer be stolen or damaged. Indeed, most of the American populace doesn't dive and may never see a wreck.

It may be perceived as a real service to our culture to remove those artifacts and preserve them, yet it requires someone with a good overview to make those decisions. It requires someone who understands the value of the wrecks and the value of the artifacts. It shouldn't be done hastily and in some cases, artifacts should never be removed from wrecks. It is a really difficult tradeoff and a really difficult decision. As a museum professional who has received artifacts here and in that way sort of endorsed their removal from wrecks, I have some real mixed feelings about it.

Do you see a change in divers' ethics toward more conservation of shipwrecks and artifacts?

Thank God, yes. Diver ethics have changed dramatically in the last few years and people are much more aware of their responsibilities to the broader public.

I think some people are still removing things. But some are deterred purely by the laws and others simply understand the real value of leaving things there. The combination of influences has made people a lot more aware and much more responsible.

Diver ethics have changed dramatically in the last few years.

What role have divers had--or will have--in bringing these important resources to the general public?

In the last 15 or 20 years a number of forums have used film and video and slide shows to bring these resources before a very large public. Effective use of various media have resulted in a better-informed public.

Today, divers can see videos of wrecks that are probably inaccessible to some divers simply because of depth. They are seeing wrecks whose locations are kept secret or wrecks that are too difficult for most divers to reach for one reason or another. Also, the average weekend diver generally doesn't have the equipment, time, and research skills to search for and find new shipwrecks. Film and video help bring that experience to many more people.

This has resulted in a number of developments. First, divers are much more knowledgeable about shipwrecks than they were 20 years ago. Much more information is available to them so they are more aware of ship construction and features. Divers are also more aware of the significance of what they are seeing on shipwrecks.

C. Patrick Labadie
Photo by Jim Montcalm

Second, there is more emphasis on hunting with a camera and obtaining good photographs of shipwrecks. Instead of concentrating on bringing back a trunkload of artifacts, divers are focusing on bringing back quality images of their underwater experiences. And that's a real wholesome change. Many divers are now using these images to carry a message of conservation.

Another result is that more people are exposed to shipwrecks. This is especially important where photography is used to bring the very deep shipwrecks to the surface. Generally, these deep wrecks are photographed by people with a real commitment to diving.

Why is the Canal Park Museum so popular?

The Canal Park Museum is one of the most popular sites in northern Minnesota. It's free and that explains it in part, but we have an average of about 430,000 visitors a year and that level has remained relatively constant since 1973. It has been gratifying to be part of such a successful museum.

What makes it successful is that three-fourths of our visitors are from metropolitan Minneapolis-St. Paul, and this is their window on Lake Superior. St. Paul is three hours from here and yet people identify with this body of water as a Minnesota Great Lakes resource. They know the story of the *Edmund Fitzgerald* so they are really attracted here to keep in touch with the lake.

It is no accident that we also provide a forum for people to watch the ships very close. You can stand here at the museum and talk to the sailors and this is one of the primary attractions. We're the only place in the Twin Ports that provides vessel schedules so we have forecasts of when the next ship is coming. The local media broadcast our schedules around the clock so people come down to Canal Park when they expect to see a ship coming.

We're at the head of the Great Lakes, the 2400-mile system that is the Great Lakes, starts right here at our footsteps and we also have that close proximity to the ship traffic as it is happening.

Do you find the general public is fascinated with shipwrecks?

Yes, it may even be a little morbid but people always have a very special fascination with shipwrecks. I'm not sure I can explain it.

I've been in the business for more than 30 years and I'm still amazed at the number of people who are really fascinated with shipwrecks. It may be a way of vicariously experiencing these life-challenging situations. Or they identify with these crew members and can only picture these experiences they went through. But it really is an interesting phenomenon because we've retired our *Edmund Fitzgerald*

I'm still amazed at the number of people who are really fascinated with shipwrecks.

exhibit three times and the public won't allow it. We keep recreating and updating it.

The *Edmund Fitzgerald* has been gone for more than 20 years and it is just as much alive today as it was 20 years ago. We have many other very dramatic losses, accidents, and storms which mark regional history yet none have been so widely publicized as the *Edmund Fitzgerald*. It has become a lightening rod for people's attention when they come here. They always want to learn more about the *Edmund Fitzgerald*.

What about the stories of gold treasure and other riches associated with shipwrecks?

There are many stories about riches lost on Great Lakes shipwrecks. That focus seemed to start with Dana Bowen's books on these shipwrecks in the 1940s. This attention has brought to light some of the most colorful shipwreck stories ever.

Many of these stories involve silver and gold and many people have the idea that these shipwrecks were frequently carrying these cargoes. Many seem to believe that it is possible to fan away a little sand to find bars of gold or barrels of whiskey for the taking.

This is, of course, a real fallacy. There were very few valuable cargoes of this nature ever on the Great Lakes. Even the items that had a great deal of value were rendered practically worthless at the time of the vessel's loss. Machinery, fabrics, furniture, and a variety of manufactured goods may have been worth much when it was loaded but water quickly destroys these items so they rapidly lose their value. In the newspaper accounts at the time of the sinking these items may have been described as valuable but they would have absolutely none of that value today.

In your research, certainly you have found that certain storms have resulted in maritime disasters. Are there any such storms that were particularly devastating?

There were some very terrible storms in the 1840s and there was a very bad one in 1869, which resulted in the loss of dozens of schooners, particularly in Lake Erie and Lake Michigan. In 1880, there was another serious storm which is usually known for the loss of the steamer *Alpena* off Holland, Michigan and several other vessels were lost in that storm.

Another serious storm occurred in 1893 and claimed dozens of watercraft around the Chicago area. Several vessels were wrecked right

The wreck of the Mataafa was witnessed by many Duluth residents.

on the Chicago shoreline.

The 1905 storm is well known here because it focused with the loss of the steamer *Mataafa*. In just 24 hours of the storm, there were 18 major steel ships lost or damaged and dozens of lives were lost in those disasters.

What does it mean when people can see a major ship loss, such as the case of the *Mataafa*?

That one was a really interesting spectacle. There was a tremendous snow storm and because of the kind of amphitheater nature of the Duluth hillsides, virtually everyone in the community could see what was happening on the waterfront.

It was customary, when there was serious storm activity, to focus on the activity at the canal. It was usually a fairly dramatic pageant with ships coming and going in the canal with heavy waves. But in that storm, in November of 1905, several ships were caught out and it was a real spectacle.

One ship was beached about a mile down Minnesota Point in full view of all of the citizens of Duluth. Later in the afternoon another vessel came in and struck the pier and sank inside the harbor. Later, the *Mataafa* came and struck the end of the piers. It sank in the lake right at the end of the piers and there was a very dramatic sequence of events that went on through the entire night. Those events went from 2:30 in the afternoon until the morning of the day following.

Thousands of people came down to the beach. They watched, tried to lend a hand, or lit fires. People were going around gathering gloves and life saving equipment but the seas were so high that nobody could render any assistance at all. Of the 24 men aboard, nine drowned or froze to death before help could get to them the following morning.

Anyone who lived through the experience of witnessing it will remember it the rest of their lives.

They were almost within shouting distance of the beach where thousands of spectators were watching--so it was a terrible feeling and anyone who lived through the experience of witnessing it will remember it the rest of their lives.

46

Does anyone come through the museum who remembers it?

We still have many people who are alive in Duluth who remember the 1905 storm. They watched it from their homes or from the beach. Many people collected souvenirs along the beach in the weeks that followed and the ship laid there all winter. It broke in half and sank in shallow water and people walked out over the ice to visit the wreck. As a result, there are hundreds of pictures of the disaster and we have dozens of them here. Remarkably, the *Mataafa* was floated off the following spring and repaired. It saw another 60 years of service.

That was only one of the 18 wrecks that were lost on that same night. Wrecks were strewn all the way up the shore and to the Apostle Islands; it was a terrible storm.

Not too many years later, in 1913, there was a storm that was just as devastating. It focused largely on Lake Huron and in 1913 the blow took about 250 lives. Like the 1905 storm, it occurred in a 24-hour period and the new steel ships of the most modern class were its most noted victims. It was horrifying.

There were other storms almost as bad in 1940, the Armistice Day Storm and individual incidents like the loss of the *Carl D. Bradley* in 1958, the *Daniel J. Morrell,* which broke up in Lake Huron in 1966, and, of course, the *Edmund Fitzgerald* in 1975.

With all of the advancements in vessel design, navigational technology, and weather forecasting, can we expect major shipwrecks in the future?

I don't believe we can ever build ships strong enough to survive all that Mother Nature can throw at them. Sooner or later the sequence is bound to start over.

I don't think we'll ever have widespread destruction like we did in some storms where underpowered ships were caught in heavy seas far from shore. Probably the most significant safety factor we have now to prevent that is accurate weather forecasts but you can bet it will happen again.

> *I don't believe we can ever build ships strong enough to survive all that Mother Nature can throw at them.*

Is there a bit of folly in thinking that ships can be made unsinkable?

People are pushing to maximize the profitability of the industry and you have to make judgements about what is safe and what isn't. Sooner or later, someone makes an error in judging the strength of the storm and the strength of the ship.

> *There are still considerable risks and eventually another major shipwreck will occur.*

And there are also equipment failures and other unforeseeable events-- engines break down and radar goes out--which result in vessels going where they don't belong.

People are generally much more informed and better prepared for emergencies these days. But there are still considerable risks and eventually another major shipwreck will occur.

How does maritime heritage fit into all of this?

There are many incentives for preserving maritime heritage. One is purely emotional. There are many people who, for a sense of identity, preserve maritime heritage as a means of becoming informed about local history. It enriches our lives to know where we came from and the background of the communities in which we live.

A second reason is the technological value of understanding how our modern way of life evolved and some of the steps through which civilization moved to arrive at our present lifestyle. In a broader sense, our maritime heritage tells us about our culture and who we are. Understanding how our culture evolved helps identify ourselves and root us as a people.

> *Our maritime heritage tells us about our culture and who we are.*

This is a small part of our history, of course, and it is a specialized focus. That is necessary because maritime trade, the maritime industry, is no longer such an important part of our lives as it was years ago. So we separate it out and look at that phase of regional history. Those of us who specialize in maritime heritage try to interpret its significance and the nature of the maritime trades of another era.

Why is it important to have a museum? Couldn't we just get this from books?

That is a really good question. It is possible to get much of this from literature and yet there isn't really any real substitute for the tangible artifact.

People want a place to come to see what these artifacts look and feel like. It isn't possible to communicate the same emotional impact to people I think through books. It might be possible through films because of the motion, because of the live action, yet there is something that is possible only with three dimensional objects--only with the real artifact.

How does this relate to diving?

Divers are in a particularly unique position to make the link between the contemporary culture and our maritime past. It is a link most seldom make.

The diver can almost do a kind of time transport and step back into the setting of a site whether it's a ship, industrial site, dock, or whatever. We seldom see these sites preserved on land and yet underwater these sites preserve a glimpse of history that is much more complete and much more valid.

Frequently, in a wreck site, we see remarkable preservation of history. Wrecks can preserve a site exactly as the ship went down. There is a tremendous emotional impact in seeing such a site and it is rarely seen with historic, terrestrial sites.

Divers are in a unique position to do an almost "time transport." Shipwreck features are preserved much better underwater than on land.

What about the link between maritime heritage and contemporary shipping?

In the museum we try to establish a link between historic and modern vessels. We try to make comparisons. People are able to see the current, ongoing activity in the Duluth Harbor and help them compare it to the photographs of the past.

In the museum we try to establish a link between historic and modern vessels.

One major difference is the technology. Between the museum and the harbor activity, one can see the evolution of sailing craft to turn of-the-century steam vessels and then to the modern electronic age.

Another major difference is scale. Ships have grown and today, when a 1,000 footer comes through here it's absolutely staggering. It is remarkable to compare the dimensions of modern 1,000-foot vessels with the 150 to 200-foot ships of 100 years ago.

What about diving wrecks? What is that experience like for you given your specialized background?

I started diving in 1960 but for a variety of reasons soon abandoned it. I didn't see where diving could help me with my research into 19th Century shipbuilding and naval architecture.

In the last few years, I've come to realize how wrong I was. There is much value in seeing the wrecks because there is an enormous store of data, in my case technological data, which simply isn't available from any other source.

Many of the details of shipbuilding technology were not recorded or if they were, they were recorded in a superficial or misleading way. We are able to fill out the historical record--to fill in the blanks--by examining the wrecks and supplementing the literature.

There is much value in examining actual wrecks. It brings to life the things I've only read about. Reading literature provides you with a skeleton and seeing the wrecks themselves provides the flesh and blood. There's that much difference.

Does shipwreck diving fill you with any special feelings because of your background knowledge?

Because of my focus on shipbuilding and naval architecture, certain kinds of landmark vessels stand out in their significance. Vessels of particular interest are those that were prototypes, first demonstrated some design feature or kind of landmark craft.

It gives me a chill to visit some of these vessels for the first time. I've read about some of these vessels for years and years and beyond the technological aspects is the human impact of seeing a wreck where you know large numbers of people lost their lives, for instance.

It gives me a chill to visit some of these vessels for the first time.

Think of the sidewheeler *Superior* at Pictured Rocks National Lakeshore. There isn't a whole lot of structure left but when you see the setting and the vessel and the handful of human artifacts left around the wreck, it's spooky. It gives you a feeling for time and the events that happened at that location. You don't have to see human remains to be affected by a site like this.

John R. Halsey, Ph.D.
State Archaeologist
Bureau of History
Michigan Department of State

John Halsey is a long-time member of Michigan's Underwater Preserve and Salvage Committee. He has seen Michigan's preserve system grow and prosper. In the process, he has encountered many issues related to Great Lakes sport diving.

Dr. Halsey is a certified scuba diver and has written extensively about Michigan's submerged cultural resources. He was interviewed about his role as Michigan's state archaeologist and management issues.

How important are shipwrecks to the state's overall history?

As the state archaeologist I am responsible for attempting to preserve archaeological sites throughout the state. Many people do not realize that 40 percent of my "coverage area" is under the waters of the Great Lakes.

The shipwrecks are an increasingly important part of our archaeological heritage because they are time capsules. I hate to use those words to describe shipwrecks because it sounds trite, but that's exactly what shipwrecks are. You have a moment frozen in time and that moment includes crew's effects, cargo, and the shipping technology that was available at that particular time. In addition, you have the actual incident itself essentially fossilized in the form of the shipwreck.

This is something that very rarely happens on land archaeological sites because many have been disturbed through the years. Of course many shipwrecks have been salvaged or otherwise disturbed but there is more potential for finding first-class undisturbed shipwrecks sites under the waters of the Great Lakes than virtually anywhere else in the country.

Shipwrecks are important because they represent the actual documentation of a major maritime and engineering technology, which was the building of a ship. So at a time when many wooden ships and early steamers were being built, this was the most complex object that society was capable of producing.

You don't see this kind of object or site preserved above water any more. Freighters, for example, if you're going to find them they're going to be on the bottom. If you want to understand the technology of how ships were built and how they were used, it is essential to have an adequate sample of ships. Those we have are those that are on the bottom of the Great Lakes.

Do divers have an impact on these historical sites?

Yes, divers do impact these sites. Divers impact them by moving artifacts around on undisturbed wrecks to take better pictures.

Even if divers don't physically disturb them, evidence of what makes many shipwreck sites important, the actual systematics of how it was lost, can be affected. We ask questions such as "Was the engine on full ahead, full astern, or dead stop?" After two or three divers have jerked on the engine telegraph lever, we'll never know exactly what that ship was doing when it went down.

For too many divers, I'm afraid the sinking of the ship and their finding it is the most important thing in the ship's life. And that's not the case. What may make the vessel important is the role the ship played in commerce, particularly the building of the Great Lakes area. How many tons of iron ore did this vessel carry? How many million board feet of lumber did it carry? How many immigrants? These are the important aspects of our maritime heritage; not the fact that it got blown over in a storm. That's just an incidental factor that led to its preservation. The real significance of a vessel lies in what it did during its working life; not its loss.

What may make the vessel important is the role the ship played in commerce, particularly the building of the Great Lakes area.

How can the state protect shipwrecks?

It's very difficult to protect these wrecks because they are essentially available to anyone who can dive them. They can be dived any time of

A diver examines one of the
boilers of the wreck of the
Cumberland in Lake Superior
near Isle Royale. Photo by
National Park Service.

the day or night. If people want to illegally dive wrecks and take artifacts, there is nothing to stop them. There are too few law enforcement officials to adequately protect them.

Realistically, the only way we'll ever be able to adequately protect them is to rely on diver ethics. We need to overcome the attitude of "If I don't take this object the next diver will." This can quickly lead to total degradation of the site as a diving experience and certainly as an archaeological site. There isn't going to be anything left to tell the story of what the shipwreck is about unless divers take the responsibility upon themselves to protect these resources.

I've often the used the phrase that shipwrecks only have one natural predator and that's the divers. If divers leave them alone--if they simply dive on them to view them, take pictures, or take measurements, which would require a certain amount of touching of the wreck--that is not a problem. What we care most about is that the artifacts be left in place and not removed. It is important that they be disturbed as little as possible so that the site, the wreck, and the diving experience is as rich for the next diver as it was for the last one.

What effect does "wreck hunting" have on these resources?

New wrecks represent the deliberate discovery of shipwrecks and this is a major problem. There is a very limited window in which to recover information about new shipwrecks.

The first four or five divers have a special responsibility. They must take a stewardship responsibility to record exactly where certain artifacts are found, especially the small, easily portable ones. They must also take responsibility for recording information that is preserved in instrument settings and dials, such as engine telegraph settings. It is important to have that information recorded, visually or on videotape, and I don't see any reason why that information cannot be preserved.

> *The first four or five divers have a special responsibility. They must take a stewardship responsibility to record exactly where certain artifacts are found, especially the small, easily portable ones.*

I understand that many of them are very deep and the amount of bottom time is limited but if the first divers don't do it, nobody else can.

Wreck hunters have actively sought out and brought these wrecks into the world. I believe they have a special responsibility--a stewardship responsibility--for seeing that the important information about it is recorded.

Should divers be restricted or prohibited from diving certain shipwrecks?

No, we don't we need to restrict divers on wrecks. I've never said that and I don't believe it's possible. I don't believe it's even desirable.

The state's position has been to encourage diving on wrecks as both a scientific activity and for recreation. There is nothing in our records at the state level that suggests we really want to restrict divers.

Some concerns have been raised by law enforcement officials. This is because it is very difficult to protect shipwrecks and they're looking for ways to protect them without unduly limiting diver access. I don't believe it will ever be possible to put wrecks off limits officially or legally. The only way that a wreck can be put off limits is for divers themselves to understand that their presence there may cause irreparable damage to the site as a diving and certainly as a historical resource.

What roles should the various parties--divers, government officials, researchers--be playing in shipwreck management?

It certainly seems to be the prevalent view in Michigan that people want to see shipwrecks preserved. Unfortunately, it is difficult to convey how to go about doing this. I don't think we really understand all the roles everyone must play, and this includes everyone from the state level to the divers to the shipwreck hunters.

It is important to recognize that there is no pressing need for shipwrecks to be discovered. We don't yet know all we need to know about the ones that are already known. Shipwrecks that have been known for 40 or 50 years are still not adequately documented and yet people go out and continue to find new ones. There really isn't a need for this. Is it illegal? No. Can we stop it? No. Does it really need to be done? No.

Can you understand the desire to "discover" a shipwreck?

Oh, yes, I can understand it. But there aren't enough shipwrecks out there for everyone who has a dream of discovering a shipwreck to discover. Sooner or later they're all going to be found. Sooner or later they're all going to be gone in the sense of being something that someone else can discover. Undiscovered shipwrecks are not an infinite resource.

I've heard it said that all we're doing is having fun, that this is a sport. Well, shooting buffalo was a sport. Hunting passenger pigeons was a sport. Shooting Aborigines in Tasmania was a sport. Passenger pigeons and Tasmanians are gone but it was a sport at the time.

> *There aren't enough shipwrecks out there for everyone who has a dream of discovering a shipwreck to discover. Sooner or later they're all going to be found.*

What about treasure hunting on the Great Lakes? Some believe some ships were carrying valuable cargoes when they were lost.

It's absolute nonsense. There are no treasure ships out there in the sense of there being gold. When it comes to stories about gold on Great Lakes ships, anything seems to become possible no matter how ridiculous or bogus the story is. People want to look for something if it can somehow be tied to a story of treasure.

There are some ships that did have valuable cargoes in the form of copper, either ingot copper or bulk copper. And some ships may have carried some items that could be salvaged. But as far as actual treasure goes, it's not there.

The real value of shipwrecks is what divers bring to the nearby communities. The value is in the money spent on lodging, restaurants, dive charters, and that sort of thing. The value is not in the removal of artifacts or from any treasure on these shipwrecks.

> **The real value of shipwrecks is what divers bring to the nearby communities.**

What kinds of cargoes were commonly transported by Great Lakes vessels?

Great Lakes ships were not carrying gold, first of all, because there is not a lot of gold in the Great Lakes area. They were carrying bulk cargoes, by and large, and sometimes package cargoes.

The cargoes consisted of iron ore, limestone, wheat, corn, a wide variety of vegetable products, and in some cases, particularly later on, manufactured goods such as knives, forks, horseshoes, nails and these sort of goods. These ships were essentially the trucks of the period at a time when the road system of the Great Lakes area was relatively undeveloped. The ships and the large piers that were built out for them in shallower water of the Great Lakes were essential to the growth of Michigan, Wisconsin, Minnesota, as economic entities. Ships have not been really understood by the public for their role in the building of the Great Lakes region.

What about shipwreck furniture makers? Is this a problem for shipwreck management?

It seems as though we have relatively few shipwreck furniture makers remaining. For those that do remain, there is an adequate supply of loose timbers in the Great Lakes to satisfy this need. Through our permitting process the recovery of isolated ship timbers and pieces of wood are available for shipwreck furniture.

I don't see this as a real problem. It's only when people want to start pulling apart existing or intact wrecks that shipwreck furniture is a

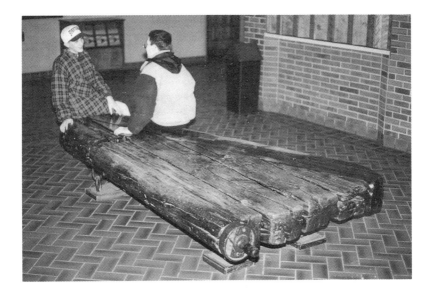

Although the state of Michigan has expressed a strong policy of protecting Great Lakes shipwrecks, one of the best collections of authentic shipwreck artifacts and shipwreck furniture can be found at Lake Superior State University in Sault Ste. Marie, Michigan. Ironically, the university is a state agency. Above is the rudder from a schooner transformed into a table. Photo by Steve Harrington.

problem. And I don't think it's only state officials who are opposed to this but the entire diving community.

How many shipwrecks are out there?

I've just come across some documentation that suggests there are many more unaccounted for ships out there than we once thought. They were lost or they just sort of disappeared from the world, particularly the smaller working vessels such as the tugboats. We simply don't know what happened to them. They may have sunk or were tied to a dock and just rotted and sank there.

Documentary records particularly for smaller vessels--those less than 100 feet long--are very poor. My belief is that there are probably many more out there to be found but they are not the kind of wrecks people generally look for. They are not big freighters or schooners. They are in the 50 to 70-foot class.

I hate to be tied to a particular number but I'd say we are probably looking at about 3,000 shipwrecks. But it is just impossible to say with much accuracy. And then we have the problem of defining what is a shipwreck. Some are virtually intact and others have been so heavily damaged in the wreck incident that there is very little left to find. A shipwreck is an incident, it's not necessarily an object or a site.

Shipwreck artifacts, such as this anchor on display at Lake Superior State University in Sault Ste. Marie, Michigan, are attractive to collectors. Photo by Steve Harrington.

Jean-Michel Cousteau
Diver/Educator

Jean-Michel Cousteau is probably best-known as the son of diving pioneer Jacques Cousteau. But Jean-Michel has been heavily involved in the production of educational materials. Most of these materials focus on the marine environment and are targeted to young adult audiences.

Jean-Michel Cousteau was aboard the Calypso when it visited the Great Lakes in the 1980s. He was interviewed about a variety of topics relating to education, diving developments, and certain Great Lakes issues.

What activities are you involved in now?

I am involved in many endeavors but one company in particular is involved in film productions, specifically, educational material productions. Right now, we are in production with nine CD ROMS. Nine CD ROMs is like producing 60 hours of film so it is an ambitious project.

Why are these educational endeavors important?

I've dedicated my life to communications. We intend to use all of the techniques available to educate people about environmental issues and the value and need for environmental protection.

It is important because there is a fundamental need to spend and manage our resources better than we have to this point so that we can preserve the quality of life for every human being on this planet.

The urgency of the matter is increasing as our population increases. It has been forecast that our population will double again in the next several years so we have to find ways to increase our productivity, better ways to manage our resources, and, hopefully, provide enough for the people that are going to be here. Fundamentally, that is the objective.

How important is it to have young people involved?

Young people are going to be either the solution-- the problem solvers of tomorrow--or the victims. And they will be the victims because of the lack of prevention and preparation for the future.

Young people have been kind of dropped out of sight by a generation of which I belong We are a very busy generation and at the same time we want a high quality of life for ourselves. With this demand it will be increasingly difficult to maintain the quality of life we expect, particularly in our industrial world. As a result of that, children are kind of drifting at a critical time when we should be guiding them and supporting them.

Young people are going to be either the solution-- the problem solvers of tomorrow--or the victims.

Unfortunately, we're not seeing the kind of family support children need. We are abandoning them in front of television sets where they gobble up hundreds of hours of garbage because they take whatever we give them. They are confused about the difference between fiction and reality and, as a result, juvenile crime is increasing.

We are at fault. The guilty are not those kids. The guilty are the generation in charge, which is us. So I'm focusing a great deal on young people and how we can help them. We must give them incentives and allow them to design their futures. At the same time you have to entertain them otherwise you lose their attention.

We must give them incentives and allow them to design their futures.

Are there any advantages in Jean-Michel Cousteau carrying that message?

To a degree there is, provided we make them understand that they are a part of the system. And what I'm doing now is getting them involved by showing them what adults are doing and saying. The message is "Come on along you are going to be the stars. You are going to be the ones designing the future for yourself and for the next generation." So we're going to feature more young people--both boys and girls--which we have never done before.

Do you have any thoughts about the *Edmund Fitzgerald*?

Visiting that shipwreck was a very emotional experience because ours were the first human eyes to go down and see for ourselves what had happened. The weather can be very treacherous, very nasty and it can turn any minute so you have windows of opportunity which are very small. And it is deep. It was spooky as a result of all of this.

Jean-Michel Cousteau
Photo by Steve Harrington

We were able to put the sub right on the bridge so we could look inside. We never found any remains unlike recent expeditions.

The ship was amazingly beautiful because it is deep and cold and nothing was growing on it and the name was still visible on the side. It was a mixture of beauty and spookiness and also a great sense of respect because of the people who had lost their lives there.

What was your personal role in that part of the expedition?

On this expedition I was in charge of security. Falco, our chief diver, was down there with one of our cameramen to film it so we could put it in one of our shows we did on the Great Lakes. I had to call the submarine back because the weather was getting bad.

What impressed you about the Great Lakes?

We didn't come up just to investigate the *Edmund Fitzgerald*. We came to the Great Lakes and the St. Lawrence River to produce two hours of film on the whole system.

I believe that when something happens at home it becomes something dear to the people at home. The *Fitzgerald* means nothing to people in Europe or in other countries. When the *Exxon Valdez* ran aground it became a big issue in the United States. Why? Because it happened in the United States. It wasn't a big issue in the rest of the world by any means. But it happened in the U.S. so the U.S. was very

63

much involved in the effort to take care of it. Had it happened somewhere else, the U.S. would have mentioned it in a small, little line in the newspaper or it would have gone completely unnoticed. So it's really a matter of where it happens and who is there at the time.

There are ships sinking all over the world all the time and you never talk about it. But that particular one was the pride of the fleet and there were a lot of newspaper stories because no cause was recorded and everyone was lost. So it becomes a big deal.

How is your father doing?

My father is like good wine. He is aging well. He will be 85 in June, which means he's not a spring chicken anymore. But he is still very active and very much involved. He is in the office six months working with the United Nations, the World Bank, and different governments and is making progress. He just keeps plugging away.

What brought your father from inventor to explorer to environmental activist?

The public only registers moments, like the creation of the aqualung or the invention--the co-invention--of the regulator. This is part of one of many steps in his life.

At the age of 13 he had a movie camera in his hand and then went into the French Navy. He had this formidable desire to explore and see what was under the ship. He started very young free diving and then proceeded to inventing cameras because there were no underwater cameras at the time, and one thing led to another.

This is part of one of many steps in his life.

Then there was the frustration of not being able to stay underwater for a long time. That's when the aqualung or scuba equipment was invented. And then he went on to something else, like underwater habitats, submersibles, and new kinds of cameras. And it never ended.

Even to this day he is inventing new things all the time. So it's not something he accomplished and put it away. He keeps doing what he wants to do and never takes "no" for an answer. If he doesn't find the equipment on the shelf because no one has created it for the specific project, he makes it. You know, your imagination is never put out of your mind and he has a very creative mind.

How old were you when you started diving?

I was seven when I was pushed overboard.

Do you remember anything about it?

No, I don't remember anything about that particular event. I grew up in that environment. It was not something that happened overnight. I saw my father playing with equipment always. It was just another piece of equipment and the time came when we could go scuba diving as a family--my brother, my late mother, my father, and myself. And we would do that when other kids were skiing in the mountains. I didn't see any difference. We were doing this and they were doing that. So there is no specific historical moment in my mind where I said, "Oh, wow! I'm doing something that nobody else is doing." or "Oh, wow! I'm a member of a family of pioneers. Nobody else is doing this." It really didn't happen that way.

What would you tell a young person who wants to learn to dive today?

First of all, I don't believe there is a limit for scuba diving. It can happen at birth. As a matter of fact, we spend nine months in liquid. So there is no limit.

Although Jean-Michel Cousteau believes there should be no minimum age to learn scuba diving, certification agencies generally set that age at 12. Photo by Steve Harrington.

The transition in a child from having no fear and starting to have fear, is a critical moment and does not necessarily happen at the same age. That is something, one must be very careful about because that is when kids start to panic and have problems. So I would be tempted to say--and I know there are rules and regulations--but the sooner the better because that fear will increase in a young child who has had a normal life.

Obviously the attention a new diver requires is formidable. And the liability and responsibilities have to come first. So it is important to be sure that the child is surrounded by the right people. And that really is a very important part; a very important issue. Some parents think they can teach their own children when they can not. I strongly advise parents that no one is a prophet in his own country or own home. It is often wise to have somebody else involved in diving instruction other than the parent.

What advice do you have for a new diver?

Have fun. That is what it is all about. And once you have time to learn about what all these creatures are, whether they are plants or animals, very quickly you have to learn to respect them.

Whether we touch or we don't touch anything, we have an impact.

You also must learn that our presence underwater has an impact. Whether we touch or we don't touch anything, we have an impact. The very fact that we are there as foreigners in the ocean will disturb the courtship or an animal protecting its young. We are an intruder. The best we can do is respect the natural world.

Harry Zych
Salvor

Harry Zych owns American Diving and Salvage in Chicago. He has been involved for many years in the salvage business. Mr. Zych also has found some of the most sought-after shipwrecks in the Great Lakes, particularly the Lady Elgin and Seabird.

But Mr. Zych's discoveries were not without controversy. He has battled state claims to artifacts he would like to raise for a traveling exhibit on maritime heritage. Both his legal battles and experience as a shipwreck hunter have made him one of the most well-known figures in Great Lakes diving.

How long have you been diving?

I've been salvaging for 26 years. I started in 1969.

My first experience was on a wooden cruiser that hit some pilings. We were coming back from a recreational dive and a gentleman asked us for some help because his boat had run aground. We dug in the sand and patched up the holes in his boat, pumped the water out and got his engine running. We were paid for the work and that was my first experience in salvaging. That was the thing that started me down the path to happiness and joy.

What kind of work does today's salvor do?

Today's salvor does a lot more than just raise boats like it was in the old days. You read the stories about Johnny Green and some of the other old time divers who raised cargo dropped from docks and primarily fixed ships that sank. The work has changed.

Today, we're asked to go out and look for things that are lost, aircraft particularly, and propellers off ships. In the old

> **Today's salvor does a lot more than just raise boats like it was in the old days.**

days, the technology was never there to find such items. We also look for lost cargoes, aircraft, boats, and instrument packages that were lost either by current or storm action. We do a wide variety of things today. It's not a fixed ship salvage business.

Is the work steady or does it vary?

It is pretty tidal. It's very cyclic. There are good times and there are bad times in any business. We are more prone to see seasonal fluctuations here in the Midwest because we have harsh winters and fairly easy summers so there's not as much demand for our services in the winter as there is in the summer.

Have you seen any major changes in salvage work in the last few years?

Oh, yes, the regulations. The government has stepped in to regulate everything from toothpaste to bobby socks. What we find is that we have laws for oil spills and hazardous materials. We have laws regarding coastal damage and we must repair beaches. And there are concerns with coastal management so that we're required to go back in if we damage the beaches in any way.

We find that we have higher insurance premiums as an outshoot of this because the regulations are so stiff. There

It seems as though every agency wants a piece of the action.

are so many requirements and now we have so many agencies to deal with that it's become a real liability issue. Salvage is no longer a simple task of taking a boat off the beach. You have to be concerned about environmental issues. It seems as though every agency wants a piece of the action.

Is there an inherent conflict between salvors and archaeologists when it comes to Great Lakes shipwrecks?

There is a tremendous conflict and it's not just strictly the salvage industry. It is the archaeologists' opinion that everything on the bottom should stay on the bottom. From our experience in raising boats, dealing with shipwrecks, and doing the kind of recovery projects that are necessary to recover property, we find that's not a realistic point of view. Everything that is on the bottom does not belong on the bottom.

There are pieces of history that only very small segment of society gets to see and those are the divers and not the general public. By recovering some of the more common and important things that are on shipwrecks, the artifacts per se, we do a service to the public by bringing these pieces of history to the general public through museum displays and exhibits.

The Lady Elgin is one of the most famous shipwrecks on the Great Lakes and was discovered by Harry Zych.

Is that your primary interest in old shipwrecks--bringing up artifacts for museum exhibits?

Absolutely. We stated from day one when I went to the government and they rejected me. We told them that our sole purpose in dealing with the *Lady Elgin* was to preserve artifacts for the public.

We felt it was one of the few historic shipwrecks in Illinois waters and what we wanted was a permanent exhibit on display somewhere in Illinois specifically related to the loss. We also wanted a traveling exhibit that would go around the Great Lakes region to various historical museums and historical societies that have contributed to maritime research. The purpose would be to enable everyone to see a piece of the *Lady Elgin*. That has been our goal since day one.

Do you remember your first Great Lakes shipwreck dive?

My first shipwreck dive was in 1969 on a schooner wrecked off St. Joseph, Michigan called the *Havana.* It was wrecked in an 1887 storm and the ship is in 50 feet of water. It is badly broken up but it had the outline of a ship even though it was flattened on the bottom to about three feet.

Here was a ship that normally would stand 12 feet off the bottom and it had been crushed by ice in a high energy zone within a mile from shore. It was busted up and broken down and only had the remnants of a ship, but it was really exciting for me.

What kinds of feelings do you have when you dive now?

I find myself filled with many concerns. I'm still excited about finding a shipwreck. It is still one of the greatest thrills you can have as an underwater explorer. You get to see something nobody else has ever seen before and it's very exciting and thrilling. It's really a feat of a lifetime.

On the other side of the coin, with all the present regulations, I'm really concerned about what is going to happen with what I've found. I'm concerned about how it is going to be treated and what may happen to me for finding it. So there is a certain amount of trepidation of government regulation and stepping into an area of absolute freedom that we have enjoyed in the past.

Now, we have some regulations and we have to live with them. It can be done but we have to have some cooperation both ways and right now it's a one-sided fence.

These shipwrecks are time capsules, true. There is

> *I'm really concerned about what is going to happen with what I've found. I'm concerned about how it is going to be treated and what may happen to me for finding it.*

archaeological and historical knowledge that's available and it's valuable to us as salvors to save that. That preserves the value of the wreck not only for ourselves but for society and that's what gives it it's real value. Not the fact that you bring something off the bottom that's 200 years old. The fact that it's recognized and historically significant--that is what the salvor really saves.

Many people have the wrong notion that salvors take massive quantities of artifacts and simply dump them on some wholesale marketplace just to make money.

Is there a marketplace for shipwreck artifacts?

Boy, I've never found it. The only market I've ever seen has been when the museums and the historical societies sell off surplus items for financing their institutions' upkeep. That is a real problem. These museums and similar organizations are underfunded.

Many of these institutions have tons of artifacts they can't afford to conserve and put on display. The cost of conservation and building an exhibit eats them up. Even the Smithsonian Institution sells surplus artifacts so, if it's a bad thing, why do they do it? The salvors are criticized for having that attitude of selling off the artifacts but in reality the museums do it for survival.

What was it like finding the *Lady Elgin*?

The *Lady Elgin* is the Holy Grail of the entire Great Lakes system. Out of all the Great Lakes shipwrecks it was listed as the second greatest disaster and, in reality, it is in second place only because the *Eastman* rolled over in the Chicago River. The Chicago River was considered a harbor but in reality it has nothing to do with the open

The Lady Elgin should be listed as the greatest Great Lakes shipwreck disaster.

waters of Lake Michigan. By rights, the *Lady Elgin* should be listed as the greatest Great Lakes shipwreck disaster. Aside from all of this, the *Lady Elgin* can still be described as the greatest open water disaster in Great Lakes history.

Tell us a little bit about the history.

The *Lady Elgin* was a 251-foot sidewheel steamer that was built in 1851. It had a colored career of accidents and mishaps but it was one of the grandest, palatial steamers of the day.

The ship's normal route was from Duluth, Minnesota down through the Soo Locks and down the west shore of Lake Michigan to Chicago. It was only a few years after the vessel was constructed that an event in

Milwaukee, Wisconsin would have a hand in her fate.

In the 1850s, the Milwaukee Third Union Guard got in trouble with the governor of the State of Wisconsin and he took away their weapons. Since the third union guard was a marching bugle corps type of band--a color guard--they participated in the 1860 Douglas rally in Chicago as a fundraiser. They hoped to earn enough money to buy new weapons.

The unit crossed on the *Lady Elgin* from Milwaukee to Chicago. When they arrived, they had an extra special good time. The unit participated in the Douglas campaign and then marched down the street. They left late at night because there were so many revelers. They were having such a great time, it is reported that some citizens mistakenly stayed on the vessel as it left Chicago for Milwaukee.

At the same time, there was a wooden schooner called the *Augustus*, which was carrying a cargo of lumber coming down the shoreline from the north. The *Lady Elgin* was heading north from Chicago and in the night the two ships collided off Highland Park. That's when the *Lady Elgin* took her death blow and she sank losing 287 people.

What about the incredible rescues involved?

The collision occurred at two o'clock in the morning and the vessel sank and broke up underneath them in 20 minutes to a half hour. The survivors rode for five to eight hours on wreckage, which was being blown toward shore. As their bad luck would have it, a violent storm came up and there was a very rough surf.

A student from Northwestern University came up the beach to aid the survivors. The surf was extremely treacherous because people were being hit by debris and others were pulled by an undertow. They had survived the collision, but many were drowning in the surf.

The survivors rode for five to eight hours on wreckage, which was being blown toward shore. As their bad luck would have it, a violent storm came up and there was a very rough surf.

This one student, Ed Spencer, went out into the surf a number of times and saved several people before he collapsed on the beach. But before he became unconscious, he asked, "Did I do my best?" That has been a credo at Northwestern University as a memorial to Ed Spencer.

Did the *Augustus* turn back?

There was a rumor at the time that the *Augustus* was intentionally sent out to ram the *Lady Elgin* and sink it because of the position of the Third Union Guard in Wisconsin. But what happened was that the *Augustus* hit the *Lady Elgin* on the port side wheelbox and the wind and waves dragged it around. The bow of the schooner acted like a can opener and laid the *Lady Elgin* open. When the wind blew the schooner down wind, it released the vessels. Because of the way the wind was blowing the crew of the schooner figured it was in worse shape than the steamer and continued sailing to Chicago.

When it got to Chicago they made an announcement that they hit some scow on the way down from the upper lakes. As it turned out, it was they who had hit the *Lady Elgin*. By that time, horrendous, terrifying stories of death and sorrow were hitting the streets by telegraph and an angry mob went to the vessel to do bodily harm to the crew.

The federal marshal came down and arrested the vessel and crew and protected them in the interim. The vessel was arrested as is normal in cases of a collision on the lake. Eventually the vessel was released and it was painted a different color and the name was changed because it was considered a black ship.

The dark history of the loss of the *Lady Elgin* doomed the *Augustus* to an unsavory title and they sailed it away and didn't bring it back. A very few years later it was lost in Lake Michigan.

How did you find the shipwreck?

I had been looking for a long, long time. I first got the bug in 1969 when I was diving with a friend on the *Havana*. He was also looking for the *Lady Elgin.*

I cut my teeth on the research portion of the project as my dues for riding on the boat to find it. It was a real interesting story and there were many interesting

> *It was such a terrific story that I got excited about it. I spent three years researching and another 17 looking for it.*

things about the people, the ship and the economic and political issues of the time. It was such a terrific story that I got excited about it. I spent three years researching and another 17 looking for it.

And when you finally found it?

There are no words to describe it.

How did you know it was the wreck?

At first, I didn't know. We were searching one of our grids in our normal search patterns and as we were searching along I had this target that was at the outside edge of the sonar screen. I looked at it and decided to get it on the next pass. But as we were continuing on the search line to complete the grid, we got another target that was bigger and better. I got excited by that and decided to take a look right away.

We turned around, came back, marked it, and got the hook over the side. I sent a crew member down to take a look at it since he'd never been the first on a shipwreck before. He swam down and came up really excited saying it had the biggest boilers he'd ever seen. When I heard that I knew there was a good chance that we had found the *Lady Elgin*.

I swam down and was very disappointed because I had no proof as to the wreck's identity. I did not have the real verification I was looking for that would confirm this was the *Lady Elgin*.

It took two or three weeks of searching the area before I found the proof that I needed. We used side-scan sonar to find the wreck but it was plain old ordinary cross-country swimming that helped us find a spoon with the name *Lady Elgin* carved in the handle.

Has the site changed much since you first dove it?

Yes, it has. It is located in a fairly high-energy zone. It is laying on a hard bottom without much sand cover so there is much wave action in big storms.

The "natural" damage is not as serious as the human damage at the site. The wreck is busted up and it's been mistreated by wind, wave, and weather but the real problem has been that the state went out to do some exploratory work in the course of litigation. They exposed it

The wreck is busted up and it's been mistreated by wind, wave, and weather but the real problem has been that the state went out to do some exploratory work in the course of litigation. They exposed it and now we have some problems with things disappearing....

and now we have some problems with things disappearing and moving around and unfortunate events like that.

Are you bitter about it?

Anyone who has fought six years in court when he was right certainly feels a little embittered. After six years there's no end in sight. But I feel that we are going to win the issue of whether we will be able to protect the rest of the site. I am also confident about winning the right to have personal property and to salvage and create this museum to bring this piece of history to the public.

Do you have any advice for new divers?

It's certainly an excellent and exciting challenge. You shouldn't run away from it.

The regulations will balance themselves out in time as people get together and find that things are unworkable as they stand today. But you should go forward, learn, grow, and participate because that's the only answer to this.

> *The regulations will balance themselves out in time as people get together and find that things are unworkable as they stand today.*

Joyce Hayward
Diver/Educator

Joyce Hayward has been diving the Great Lakes for recreation for many years. She is an enthusiastic supporter of many diving organizations, such as the Ohio Council of Skin and Scuba Diving and she is a member of the Association for Great Lakes Maritime Heritage.

Joyce is also an accomplished underwater photographer and her entertaining and informative programs have been shown at major diving events throughout the region. When not diving, Joyce teaches elementary school near Bellevue, Ohio.

Of all the types of diving you have done--tropical and Great Lakes--which is your favorite?

Shipwreck diving is absolutely my favorite. That was made clear to me during a very unique experience.

I was part of a team diving a shipwreck that went down off the Florida Keys in 1622. It sank with about $400 million in gold treasure. The treasure was all still there when we were diving but it was a very unusual experience.

When I got in the water I really thought it would be the excitement of seeing the treasure that would impress me the most. But there was something more powerful than that.

When I saw the shipwreck for the first time, I touched the wood of that ship and it was like going back in time. And I remembered when I was in school studying about Spanish galleons and Pizzaro and Cortez. Being there, on that ship so many years later, just gave me the feeling of those people. There was the thought that they could have been on that ship long before it sank. It was almost like their presence was still there.

That is something I notice when I dive on Great Lakes shipwrecks-- the memory of the past people. There are the memories of the people who built the ship and the people who sailed on them. It's that feeling that makes these shipwrecks very special and important to me.

Another great experience is visiting a ship under construction. There aren't very many places where you can see wooden ships being built. There are a few museums that want to keep the feeling and the understanding of the old wooden ships being built so they have demonstrations. They had one in Maine I went to see one time. It helps you understand what you're looking at on the bottom a little bit better.

Do you have a preference as to the kind of shipwrecks you dive?

Wooden ships are more interesting to me. When I am scuba diving I have a very close feeling for those vessels. They were built by hand, and sailed by hand. These ships were very special and important to the people who built and worked on them and I feel that when I'm diving these wrecks.

Wooden ships are more interesting to me.

But the steel ships have much to offer, too. It is really interesting to visit the *Valley Camp*, which has been developed into a maritime museum in Sault Ste. Marie. Some of the ships we dive are very similar to the *Valley Camp*.

Of the Great Lakes, which is your favorite for diving?

My favorite place to dive is Lake Superior. The water is cold but it's very clear and there are some fantastic shipwrecks, especially in areas such as Isle Royale.

Why do people get into diving?

My favorite place to dive is Lake Superior. The water is cold but it's very clear and there are some fantastic shipwrecks.

People start diving for a variety of reasons. Someone in the family or friends have an interest in it or perhaps interest is sparked by watching a television program. I'm pretty typical of those who just suddenly say "Come on, let's give it a try."

What is so special about Great Lakes diving?

Many people are attracted to warm-water diving because of beautiful coral and fish and I have a lot of interest in that, but my real love is shipwreck diving in the Great Lakes. Our ships are so much more intact and I get a feeling of history when I'm diving on them--the presence of mankind.

There is also an educational element. The first time I dove a wooden shipwreck I didn't know

Joyce Hayward, left, discusses diving with Nick Burnett while strolling on a Lake Huron beach. Photo by Jason Harrington.

anything about it. I could see the recreational value but I knew there was a lot more. There was the history to learn, there was the construction of the ship, there was the story of the people and why they were sailing on the ship, why it went down. And then, of course, understanding the construction of the ship also has its appeal to me.

Why are you so dedicated to presenting slide shows and programs to nondivers?

I guess it's the teacher in me wanting to show others what I've seen. I like to tell the story of a ship. Sometimes, if it's a program for a group of sport divers, I like to do the underwater photography on the shipwreck and a travelogue to tell folks what they're going to be seeing along the way.

Underwater photography is an excellent opportunity to share what I am seeing with not only a diving audience but with those who are nondivers as well. Nondivers seem to have just as great an interest as the divers, perhaps from a different aspect, but there is that natural curiosity about what the ship looks like when it is a shipwreck and the story behind it.

Most nondivers are totally amazed at the water clarity we have here in the Great Lakes. They are also surprised to see that the ships are intact and the story that goes with them is also interesting.

What aspect of recreational diving is the most recreational for you?

It's a lot of fun, especially the comraderie. One thing I've noticed about my friends, my diving friends, is that these are much more lasting and serious friendships than my skiing friends or my friends who are involved in other recreational activities. We are each others' support system and there is the interest that we have to share with one another. It's a lot of fun but there's more to it than that.

> *We are each others' support system and there is the interest that we have to share with one another. It's a lot of fun but there's more to it than that.*

How can you use diving with education?

In a variety of ways. The marine biology is a good example. I start my fourth grade science class with a unit on oceanography, which they just love. I've carried a salt water tank into my room and gotten that started and, of course, kids just love the scuba gear.

The school children get really excited when they find out I dive. There's just something about the fact that their teacher is a scuba diver that perks their interest up. And then I'm able to tie my experiences to photography, and the saltwater tank in my classroom.

All this just brings science a little more alive than simply opening a textbook and saying we're going to read about something in the ocean.

Why should young people learn to dive?

Diving can open the door to a world of wonderful experiences for young people. They can watch the personalities of the fish and see for themselves how the fish behave and the interaction between them. It will give them a true love of the ocean and from that they will want to understand and learn more about it.

All of that applies to the Great Lakes, plus there are the shipwrecks.

The experience of learning how to dive puts young people into such an exciting environment. It is one thing to read about ecology and history, but diving can bring these alive and last them for a lifetime.

Is there something about the diving experience that is especially appealing?

The diving experience is very very pleasurable, especially the weightlessness. I have a very good friend I started diving with who is in a wheelchair. I watched the freedom he experienced getting out of that wheelchair and just floating effortlessly along the bottom or along a shipwreck. It helps me have a real appreciation for the actual diving experience.

Joyce Hayward and Nick Burnett discuss
diving issues. Photo by Jason Harrington.

Through the years, have you seen a change in sport diving ethics?

I'm personally very pleased with the change of ethics of sport divers through the years. Maybe it's because as an educator or as a parent, I'm really glad that sport divers are taking the attitude of leaving the ships alone--not removing artifacts--and leaving them so they look like ships.

Here, in the Great Lakes, we have excellent preservation in the freshwater and I would like those ships to look the same for me as they look for the next generation and the following generation. Only if we leave the ships alone will they be there for the children to see later.

Just in the years I've been diving I've seen a real change. And it seems like it's a growing change. It's respect for the children, our

children and maybe even our grandchildren so they can see these
shipwrecks we're seeing now.

Frederick J. Shannon
Great Lakes Explorer

A scuba diver since 1969, Frederick Shannon has become known as a Great Lakes explorer, and for good reason. In 1994, he led a record-setting expedition to Lake Superior to explore the remains of the Edmund Fitzgerald. In 1995, he explored the shipwreck of the Carl D. Bradley in northern Lake Michigan.

Mr. Shannon plans to continue exploration in the Great Lakes and believes there are many exciting discoveries yet to be made. Although his expeditions were once viewed with apprehension and suspicion, he has proven to himself and others that for those willing to make personal sacrifices, almost anything is possible.

What is a Great Lakes explorer?

There are few real explorers left. They are the ones who set out to make new paths. The Great Lakes are largely unexplored. Only 1/16 of the Great Lakes bottomland has been mapped so there is much room for discovery. I see the Great Lakes as a great treasure for those who want to be the first to see new things, new places.

For many years, I thought the Great Lakes were places that offered little for exploration. But diving opened my eyes. I now know there is more to find and much lies beneath the water. The Straits of Mackinac is a good example. When we dove in a submarine we discovered fantastic limestone formations.

How do you decide where to explore?

As a diver, I was frustrated because I couldn't reach many deep sites. With a submarine, we can easily reach and explore shipwreck sites such as the *Edmund Fitzgerald, Carl D. Bradley*, and *Daniel J. Morrell*.

Exploring these shipwrecks is fascinating because they are similar to crime scenes. In many cases, we know something happened, but we don't know why. In that way, I am like an underwater detective and through pictures and videos, I bring the crime scene to the surface.

Experts and others can see the evidence for themselves and determine the cause of the wreck.

Are you just interested in shipwrecks?

Not at all. The Great Lakes have many interesting geological formations and people frequently report to me unknown targets they find on their sonars. These are areas of mystery. They may be caves or something entirely new and, as yet, undiscovered. These are the type of areas that interest me.

It is exciting to explore and solve mysteries. Sometimes these targets turn out to be just large rocks, but there is always that anticipation. There is always excitement with every submarine dive.

What drives you to spend the time and money and take the risks to explore?

There is a certain passion to be first. I like to be the first to see new things and make discoveries. The Great Lakes are a place where one can go and see things that no other human has ever seen. They are unique in that way and I am simply taking advantage of the exploration opportunities.

There is a certain passion to be first.

You have been at the center of controversies regarding your exploration activities. Do those controversies bother you?

Controversies are irrelevant. I am not out to please anyone or any group. I am exploring and history shows that explorers have their critics. As a result, they are always the subject of controversy. If you look at Columbus, Peary, and Byrd and the controversies they spawned, I'm in pretty good company.

I am a bit bothered, however, by the intent of some critics. Obviously there are those who use controversy in an attempt to

I am exploring and history shows that explorers have their critics.

thwart discovery. That is a dangerous mindset because it is human desire to discover, to explore, that makes us unique. In the United States, that very spirit is important because in many respects, our country was founded by those willing to try new things--willing to discover.

Frederick Shannon prepares to descend for exploration of the Edmund Fitzgerald in Lake Superior. Photo courtesy of DeepQuest Publishing, Ltd.

If we let critics thwart discovery, then we must forego all scientific discoveries. That means we are doomed as a civilization to repeat mistakes and tolerate such diseases as AIDS, tuberculosis, smallpox, and polio. I am not willing to accept that attitude. I am going to continue regardless of controversy.

Do your activities interfere with other endeavors, such as archaeological research?

Not at all. Some archaeologists have called and asked if I was somehow bent on destroying archaeological sites. Nothing could be further from the truth. I have invited archaeologists and others fearful of my activities to join me. The question raises an important point. We must look carefully at the role of explorers in our own backyard.

Because my expeditions are privately funded, I have no formal guidelines to follow. No government, no professional association, and no critic can control most of my activities. Instead, I have responsibilities, a code of ethics, derived from my own experience and the experience of other explorers.

That code of ethics means that I must not hurt others and I must share my experiences. Through presentations, I share the results of my explorations. Anyone can come and see what I saw. They can participate in the exploration themselves by sharing the experience through photos and video. Through this sharing, knowledge that can be obtained in no other way is passed along. In this way, by learning from our successes and failures, we are helping future generations push other envelopes.

Some have criticized you because you operate as a for-profit corporation. Are you making money unfairly?

There is no shame or embarrassment in attempting to recoup losses sometime in the future. These expeditions are extremely expensive and I've mortgaged my home and borrowed money to finance them. I simply cannot continue without financial support of some sort.

Ironically, there is really very little practical difference between exploring as a profit corporation or as a nonprofit corporation. We can do the same things but as a nonprofit corporation we would have access to public funds. I refuse to do that. True exploration should not be done at the public trough. Private financing provides me with tremendous independence and while there are many public benefits to what I do, the taxpayer does not have to pay for those benefits.

These expeditions are extremely expensive and I've mortgaged my home and borrowed money to finance them.

Besides your own pocket, where does your funding come from?

It seems as though I am always fundraising. We get many private donations, some small and some substantial. People pay for presentations, and we sell T-shirts, coffee mugs, videos, books, and pictures. In this business, you have to wear many hats to survive.

But there is more to it than simply fundraising for the next expedition. Through the presentations, we share our experiences and help others learn. We also inspire others to reach out and test their own limits. And by contributing financially, people who would otherwise be unable to participate can do so vicariously. The person unable to be there physically can enjoy his or her participation through news reports of the expeditions. They know that, through their financial support, they are truly part of the expedition, and we don't forget that.

What about failure?

Failure is an inherent risk of exploration. That is especially true when we are dealing with something as unpredictable as the Great Lakes. During our 1995 expedition to the *Carl D. Bradley*, for example, we had several days of heavy seas that kept us off site. On the last day we finally succeeded in reaching the wreck, but failure is always possible, if not probable. One must remember that not everyone climbs Mt. Everest or swims the English Channel on the first try. If it were easy, everyone would be doing it.

We do all we can, through comprehensive planning, to reduce the risk of failure. But even the most detailed planning cannot account for bad weather and certain mechanical problems.

It is also important to recognize that it is through failure that we learn. While much can be learned from success, much more is often learned from failure. Failure teaches us what not to do and it also challenges our creativity and resolve. Failure can teach us not only about how to accomplish a particular task, but also about ourselves.

What role have young people played in your expeditions?

We have started an educational program for young people. We believe it will grow to become a major part of what we do.

I was amazed that our group of nine students were so interested in

The Delta Submarine used by Frederick Shannon in his exploration of the Great Lakes. Courtesy of DeepQuest Publishing, Ltd.

all of the activities. They sat for hours talking with scientists, technicians, and historians. The living conditions were less than ideal but they didn't seem to mind. They were there for the experience.

The education program started with a presentation by a Great Lakes ecologist. They covered a variety of topics related to water quality and the dynamics of the Great Lakes ecosystem. That was followed by actual experience on the water. It was a powerful teaching and learning opportunity. We hope to find the funding to continue this part of the program and perhaps expand it so we can prepare young people with experiences that will enable them to tackle tough problems in the future.

What are your plans for the future?

There are many places in the Great Lakes to explore. There are major shipwreck sites, of course, but there are also places like the deepest parts of each of the Great Lakes. I would like to go down 1,300 feet in Lake Superior and see what is there. While we are there, we could sample the water and soils for university studies. Perhaps even high schools would be interested in using samples for classroom teaching and experiments.

There are some fascinating geologic formations off the Keweenaw Peninsula. We understand, for example, that unique copper formations are found off the peninsula and Isle Royale. We also understand that some unscrupulous divers and others are removing those formations for profit. It would be valuable to photograph and videotape those formations before they are lost forever.

There are airplanes in Lake Michigan, cargo spills, reefs, and underwater forests. I also have a notion that, somewhere, there is an underwater Native American village to discover.

There is no shortage of places to explore.

There is no shortage of places to explore. The only questions as to whether that exploration will occur are financial. I've shown that I have the resolve. I fully intend to continue probing the Great Lakes as long as I can.

Steve Harrington
Diver/Author

Steve Harrington has been diving and writing about diving for many years. In addition, he has conducted research and prepared reports for various state and federal agencies on submerged cultural resources.

But more than anything, Steve loves to share his passion for diving with others. He often helps new divers become accustomed to Great Lakes shipwreck diving. Steve is an attorney and environmental consultant and lives in St. Ignace, Michigan, where he is close to many of his favorite dive sites.

> *Do not burn yourselves out. Be as I am--a reluctant enthusiast ... a part-time crusader, a half-hearted fanatic. Save the other half of yourselves and your lives for pleasure and adventure. ...keep your brain in your head and your head firmly attached to the body, the body active and alive, and I promise you this much: I promise you this one sweet victory over our enemies, over those desk-bound people with their hearts in a safe deposit box and their eyes hypnotized by desk calculators. I promise you this: you will outlive the bastards.*
>
> --Edward Abbey

We could go on and on about what is wrong with Great Lakes diving. We could talk about potential regulations and how they may or may not affect the sport. And we could talk about all the work ahead of us to do what is right for the sport. Instead, it seems more important at this time to focus on what is <u>right</u> about Great Lakes diving.

There is an untold story of how volunteers have proven their abilities to manage and protect our most fragile resources. Their stories are shining examples of how these resources can be managed without pricey budgets and well-organized, government endeavors.

In each of the underwater preserves, and in a few coastal communities without preserves, there are groups of volunteers. For lack of a better title, these groups are often referred to as "community support organizations." But that name does little to describe the work performed unselfishly by dedicated Great Lakes divers.

There is an untold story of how volunteers have proven their abilities to manage and protect our most fragile resources.

Although many of these accomplishments occur in Michigan's underwater preserves, there are groups of volunteers in each Great Lakes state performing important tasks. Here are a few examples:

Mooring Buoys are placed at popular diving sites throughout the underwater preserves--and elsewhere--by volunteers. The buoys, chain, line, and hardware were generally purchased through grants from the Coastal Zone Management Program. But each year the buoys must be placed on the wrecks, monitored, and then retrieved before winter.

It can take several dives to secure a single buoy to a shipwreck. The task is often complicated when the forces of nature or a freighter has destroyed or damaged the buoy system. Throughout the summer diving season, divers must monitor the system for wear or loss. And in the fall, divers must again visit each buoy and prepare the system for winter.

The buoys do much more than simply offer convenience. They protect shipwrecks by avoiding the need to grapple shipwrecks or drop an anchor. Both of these devices are known to tear apart the very resources divers enjoy.

Another benefit is the appeal to divers new to the area. Michigan's underwater preserves attract divers from throughout the United States and one reason is the convenience of locating dive sites. Gone is the guesswork generally associated with finding a shipwreck and the risk of securing a diving vessel at the site.

Inventories--While many still enjoy searching for new shipwrecks, it is undeniable that we have yet to obtain a complete understanding of shipwrecks that have been known and explored by divers for many years.

Steve Harrington

Slowly, almost painstakingly, we are obtaining that understanding. In some cases, professional maritime archaeologists are performing research and documentation, such as the amazingly productive David Cooper of the Wisconsin Historical Society. Cooper has trained a strong contingent of volunteer divers who ably assist him.

In many other cases, volunteer divers are taking the lead in researching and documenting shipwrecks. For some, such as Mike Spears of Dearborn, Michigan, the challenge has resulted in much more than detailed life histories of wrecked vessels, but also computer-aided drawings that carry all the authority of professional archaeology. Spears has created slide shows that share this knowledge with divers and other maritime historians.

Valerie Olson, of Twin Lake, Michigan, deserves special credit for her contributions in the form of detailed shipwreck drawings as does Pat Stayer of Lexington, Michigan.

Other sources of inventory work include Michigan Sea Grant and research project funded, in part, by the Coastal Management Program of the Michigan Department of Environmental Quality. Generally, these inventories are created in conjunction with underwater preserve designation in Michigan.

Recreational divers can obtain specialized training in maritime archaeology through museums, dive clubs, and other organizations. And British Columbia has published a comprehensive guide to help divers document shipwrecks on their own.

As a result, we have a growing body of information that is quickly allowing us to better understand the importance of our maritime pasts. But much work still remains. By some estimates there are thousands of shipwrecks to document as well as dock ruins and other submerged cultural sites. In some cases, such as the Straits of Mackinac Underwater Preserve, the information is used to create shore access dive sites that can be enjoyed by divers, who, for a variety of reasons, are unable or unwilling to enjoy boat diving.

For divers interested in protecting history and making real contributions to historical preservation, real opportunities abound.

> *We have a growing body of information that is quickly allowing us to better understand the importance of our maritime pasts.*

Books and Brochures--All the information in the world is useless unless it is shared. Fortunately, there is a growing number of books and brochures that complement the growing information base.

These books and brochures, for the most part, are intended to make Great Lakes diving easier and more enjoyable. They contain maps and coordinates of key dive sites, which greatly increases access. No longer must divers barter or pay for information about where the "best" shipwrecks are located. Instead, literature can be found to assist them.

All the information in the world is useless unless it is shared.

Other publications, such as this one, are less oriented to facilitating diving access and are more focused on issues of vital concern to diving. These publications focus on important debates that could affect diving for generations to come.

Fortunately, dive retailers have come to realize the importance of these publications and most now offer many titles to entertain and inform divers between dives.

A diver once came to me at a dive show and, as he vigorously shook my hand, told me how *Divers' Guide to Michigan* had changed his life. At first I was amused. How could such a book really make a significant difference to anyone? But then I thought about the uncertainties I faced when I began diving. That dark water can be intimidating!

Books and brochures help break that barrier. They provide information that bolsters security and helps others follow--even if the path is well worn.

Videos and Slide Shows--As stated before, information is virtually useless unless it is distributed. Videos and slide shows have become tremendously effective communicating that information. Underwater video recorders and still cameras have become more reliable, convenient, and inexpensive. This combination has resulted in a proliferation of divers using these devices.

Videos and slide shows have become tremendously effective communicating that information.

But what divers do above water with their videos and photos is every bit as important

92

VERANO

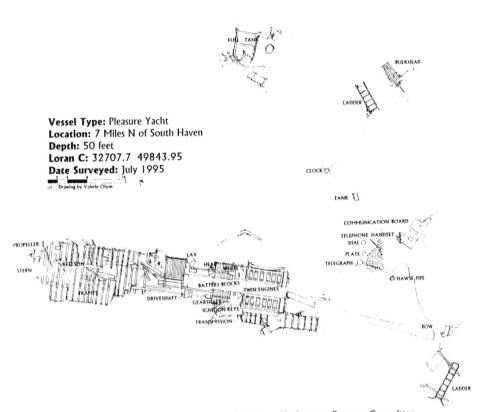

Vessel Type: Pleasure Yacht
Location: 7 Miles N of South Haven
Depth: 50 feet
Loran C: 32707.7 49843.95
Date Surveyed: July 1995

Drawing by Valerie Olson

Southwest Michigan Underwater Preserve Committee

Drawings of shipwreck sites, such as this one by Valerie Olson, help divers understand and feel more comfortable about Great Lakes shipwreck diving.

as what they do underwater. Through these images, divers are discovering a ready means of sharing their underwater world with others.

In many cases, divers create elaborate productions for small to large groups of divers. In other instances, divers simply share their raw footage and photos with friends and neighbors. In both cases, divers are effectively using images captured underwater to "take" nondivers with them.

This sharing is extremely important. First, we must remember that maritime history is not the sole domain of divers and there are many more nondivers than divers. To some extent, nondivers have an inherent "right" to share in this history and shipwrecks and dock ruins represent an important component of that history. Through this sharing, nondivers become very real participants in maritime history appreciation.

Second, if maritime history is allowed to become the exclusive domain of divers, then divers run this risk of increased regulation and even resourcc loss as nondivers clamor to "touch history" through submerged artifacts.

In this way, divers have done much more than preserve their sport. They bring maritime history to the surface where large numbers of people can enjoy and learn from it.

My father has never strapped on a tank or even a mask. Yet it is he I must credit for my underwater adventures. He taught me the value of exploration and facing challenges. It is he who taught me to wonder about what lay below.

Videos and photographs are my "trophies." It is through these images that I share my adventures with my father. It is through these adventures that we share a common sense of accomplishment and understanding. And through this understanding of the underwater world we understand each other.

> *If maritime history is allowed to become the exclusive domain of divers, then divers run this risk of increased regulation and even resource loss as nondivers clamor to "touch history" through submerged artifacts.*

Ethics have changed dramatically in the last two decades. There was a time when the success of a dive was measured by the number of artifacts retrieved from a shipwreck.

For those of us who have been Great Lakes diving a long time, it would be convenient to say we have never removed a spike, porthole, or other artifact to "remember" the dive. But that is a lie. It is better for us to "come clean" and acknowledge our wrongs.

One quiet, late-summer evening, I made a lonely voyage to a remote location in the Manitou Passage. It was only myself, the moon, and a reflection upon the water. I let the outboard of my small boat sputter to a stop and then it was only me, my thoughts, and a handful of small artifacts. As the boat drifted over a particular shipwreck, I watched as the rusting iron and tarnished brass slid into the water and "home" from whence they came.

Archaeologists may say I had jeopardized the integrity of the site by returning the artifacts and some divers may say the act was futile

New divers see shipwrecks and other underwater features with "fresh eyes" that make diving exciting for all. Photo by Steve Harrington.

because the artifacts would only be stolen by the next group of divers. I don't know and I'm not sure I really care.

All I really know is that it felt good. It felt as though a wrong had been righted. It felt as though bits of history had returned to where they belonged.

We have changed--us old divers. For the most part we know that unless we lead the way, shipwrecks will disappear piece by piece. I have seen it happen.

No, my hands are not entirely clean. I cannot say that I have never removed an artifact. But I can say I have made mistakes and learned from them. Why do I feel this way? Read on.

New Divers are special--especially young divers. Through their eyes we "old" divers can see the excitement of discovery, exploration, and adventure.

It was at a public hearing for the designation of the Manitou Passage Underwater Preserve that I really came to understand what before I had only felt was right. Adults had crammed into a tiny meeting room to speak into a microphone and have their testimony recorded by state officials. After the adults had spoken, 13-year-old Nate Morgan, who had accompanied me to the hearing, stood up to speak. Odd as it may seem to some, there is not a dive season that I do not remember his words.

"Steve promised he would take me diving on some of these shipwrecks," Nate said in a strong and sure voice. "I want there to be something left for me to see."

Nate is now a grown man and married. But his youthful words spoke a certain truth that remains with me today. In his words, he was telling us that we have a duty to keep these shipwrecks intact. And when we take even the most insignificant souvenir the theft is felt not so much by us as it is the next generation--the divers yet to come.

Yes, Nate learned to dive and together we explored shipwrecks of the Manitou Passage and many others. And there have been other new divers who have taught me the value of shipwreck conservation.

When we take even the most insignificant souvenir the theft is felt not so much by us as it is the next generation--the divers yet to come.

More and more I have come to realize that we "old" divers have a duty to save shipwrecks and that duty may extend beyond resource protection. It is a duty I have come to embrace because it has made me a better diver--one who thoroughly enjoys the sport.

Through the years, I have "mentored" more than a dozen new divers--many young and some not-so-young. This mentoring keeps me "in touch," it helps me keep my head on straight by reminding me that other divers follow and I have an important reponsibility to them.

Experienced divers who make the effort to share the sport with others know how to keep feelings of excitement, exploration, and adventure alive. I hope that, as I enter my third decade of diving, I never lose those feelings. I hope I never run out of new divers to mentor. And I hope other experienced divers learn to take time to dive slower, shallower, and more carefully with new divers. Finally, I hope they learn to share the joy of diving with a generation certain to face challenges we have yet to imagine.

Michelle Malarney
NOAA Marine Sanctuaries

Michelle Malarney was hired by the National Oceanic and Atmospheric Administration (NOAA) of the U.S. Department of Commerce, to determine the feasibility of a national marine sanctuary at Thunder Bay in Lake Huron. Ms. Malarney began her work in 1991 and the project has undergone many transformations since.

The following is taken from a presentation made to an environmental group at Lake Superior State University in October 1995. Questions were posed by the audience, a group of nondivers. NOAA declined to cooperate in the publication of this material and many divers complain that they have been left out of the marine sanctuary designation process.

Fourteen areas, all in oceans, have been designated national marine sanctuaries. These sanctuaries are found in the coastal waters of the United States and its tributaries. The sanctuary program is strictly a water-based program although benefits accrue to terrestrial plants and animals.

The three primary purposes of national marine sanctuaries are 1) resource protection, 2) research and education, and 3) environmental education and technology transfer. We consider a variety of factors in determining feasibility, including historical significance because the program covers submerged cultural resources.

In the early 1980s a list of candidate areas was developed by NOAA. A site evaluation list was narrowed down to five sites: Traverse Bay, Green Bay, Apostle Islands, Sandusky Bay, Cape Vincent, and Thunder Bay. In 1991, only Thunder Bay near Alpena was made an active candidate to consider for feasibility. Currently, we are looking at 700 square nautical miles as a potential sanctuary.

NOAA is in the process of developing an environmental impact statement and a management plan. These will consider natural and

97

cultural resources as well as environmental conditions. It is interesting to note that the area hosts interesting geological formations such as 90-foot deep sinkholes.

NOAA will also examine various human activities such as recreation in the form of fishing and sport diving as well as industries. Many research activities are already being performed in the Thunder Bay area, such as zebra mussel research by the University of Michigan.

Thunder Bay hosts more than 130 shipwrecks with the most recent being that of the *Nordmeer* in the 1960s.

Why is Thunder Bay being considered for national marine sanctuary designation?

Originally, NOAA was asked to consider the area due to the interest expressed by the community. There was a vision that the area could become an underwater park of sorts with a variety of services. The state is unable to fund the preserve program and local residents were hopeful that a marine sanctuary could bring in funds to promote tourism in the region.

State officials are wary because of a history of problems with federal-state partnerships.

NOAA was asked to consider feasibility by local residents. State officials are wary because of a history of problems with federal-state partnerships. We will be looking at all issues pertaining to cooperation between local, state, and federal governments and tribal units.

What would be the purpose of a sanctuary?

Here, we have decided to focus only on underwater cultural resources. There was a loud outcry from sport and commercial fishermen and industry when we looked at other issues. They believed, and NOAA agrees, that existing regulations already adequately protect the environment in this area. As a result, we are focusing only on shipwrecks, dock pilings, and other submerged cultural resources.

We are focusing only on shipwrecks, dock pilings, and other submerged cultural resources.

The purpose of a NOAA marine sanctuary would be to increase awareness and understanding of underwater cultural resources. We need to address the needs of those who do not dive and that may be done through glass-bottom boats, videos, a maritime museum, and a Great Lakes education center. Currently, a separate study is being conducted by Michigan State University to examine the feasibility of a Great Lakes education center for the area.

How would the marine sanctuary address maritime heritage issues?

NOAA would address these issues from a very broad perspective. Although the sanctuary would be a water-based program, we would be looking at maritime heritage to include the role of lighthouses. What we would like to do is examine the role of maritime history, of the shipwrecks, and explain the relationship between the natural resources and shipwrecks. We want to explain why the ships are there and why that is important.

Would this mean additional regulations?

It could, although we would be encouraging multiple uses. Basically, we hope to simply mirror existing state laws, which protect these resources well. This would be like "resource sharing" where the federal government could come in with funds to work on the education perspective. In some marine sanctuaries resource protection has meant site closure and inhibition of certain activities.

In some marine sanctuaries resource protection has meant site closure and inhibition of certain activities.

Why would NOAA duplicate state efforts?

The preserve program is not funded. This is a way to bring in the federal government with more money to address education issues. Also, we may be able to find additional shipwrecks. Only a relatively small number of the 130 shipwrecks known to be in the area have been found.

This is community-driven. They, the Alpena-area community, now want to capitalize on their local resources to bring in tourists. The whole purpose would be to bring in additional tourists to the area.

The role of NOAA and state and local entities is still undefined. That is what we are working on now, to find out what every unit can and should do.

What kind of staffing are we looking at for a marine sanctuary?

Federal budgets are declining so there would be minimal staffing at first. We are looking at one sanctuary manager and an education coordinator to start.

You have been working on this project for more than four years. What are you doing?

All major industries have been involved in the process. We are now writing the environmental impact statement and the management plan. We hope to have those available soon, but we have had those hopes for years.

We still have yet to define what a marine sanctuary would be. It is too early for support or opposition. This would be the first sanctuary in state waters so the relationships between governments must be worked out.

Who would oppose such a sanctuary?

We've had opposition from various industries and fishing groups. They were very vocal in their criticism so we decided it would be best to focus only on the submerged cultural resources.

We still have some tribal and industrial opposition. And some diving groups are opposed to the proposed sanctuary. Most opposition fears additional federal regulation but the environmental impact statement would define the scope of regulatory involvement. The state would still own the bottomlands and the resources. It would be a co-management sort of agreement.

Divers are opposed to federal involvement because diving can be prohibited in a marine sanctuary.

Divers are opposed to federal involvement because diving can be prohibited in a marine sanctuary. We do not expect to have those kinds of regulations although we would probably have regulations concerning petroleum exploration and endangered species protection.

Are you saying that you are down to submerged cultural resources only because divers have not been sufficiently vocal in their opposition?

No. We are not listening to divers alone. We are listening to a variety of interest groups so even if divers are strongly opposed, the sanctuary may still be designated.

We are listening to a variety of interest groups so even if divers are strongly opposed, the sanctuary may still be designated.

How much money has been spent so far?

In a little more than four years we have spent between $350,000 and $400,000.

And what do you have to show for it so far?

We are in the process of writing our environmental impact statement and management plan. If there is no significant opposition to those, we will proceed to negotiate an agreement with the state.

We have missed several deadlines for these documents but now we have a graphic artist working on the project so I'm sure we will have these documents ready soon.

Some state officials have said they will oppose any agreement that does not include a sunset provision. Will your management plan contain such a provision?

A sunset provision is one that sets a time limit on a program to evaluate its effects. No, the documents we are preparing will not contain a sunset provision. We will see if the state will accept a sanctuary without a sunset when it comes to negotiations.

Do you believe this area will eventually be designated?

That is a good question. We believe the environmental impact statement and management plan will reflect a considerable amount of thought and input from

NOAA Marine
Sanctuary Logo

diverse groups.

Still, there is legitimate concern about another state-federal partnership. There is a history of problems and perhaps now is not the time for another relationship of that sort.

Since Malarney's presentation, the federal government has been "shut down" twice. In addition, fees for national parks have been increased approximately 400 percent. Some divers now believe a marine sanctuary would result not only in the outright prohibition of diving on some shipwrecks, but would jeopardize diving in sanctuaries during times of government shutdowns. Also, stiff fees have been proposed for diving in marine sanctuaries in the past. Some wonder if those fees are very far in the future.

Michael Neuman
Diver/Historian

The following article by Michael Neuman appeared in many newspapers throughout the Midwest. We requested that it be reprinted here because it reflects considerable thought, is well written, and demonstrates how divers, and others, can contribute to the debate about various diving issues.

Mr. Neuman is a diver and member of the Association for Great Lakes Maritime Heritage. He lives in Traverse City, Michigan.

The recent attention given the salvage of the bell from the *Edmund Fitzgerald* has raised the issue of whether to make the site off-limits to further exploration.

Explorers have visited the *Fitzgerald* wreck on several occasions, taken many still photographs, and produced a number of video tapes. Their apparent ambition is to profit from these ventures in the form of books sales, videotape sales, speaking engagements, or by using the ship's bell as a public draw. Such endeavors are generally cast in a favorable light (consider the exploits and popularity of Jacques Cousteau and Robert Ballard). However, the possibility of future expeditions to this specific wreck site is drawing an unusual amount of critical attention.

I feel much sympathy for the families and friends of the victims of not only the *Edmund Fitzgerald,* but of all Great Lakes shipwrecks. Their loss is made more difficult because of the high profile nature of shipwreck disasters. Though taking the ship's bell from the *Fitzgerald* wreck may help to bring closure to the grief still felt by the victim's loved ones, the motives of the principles involved must be questioned.

The presentation of the bell to the victims' relatives garnered much publicity and was a considerate gesture, but in truth, the bell will remain under the direct control and possession of the party responsible for

> **The motives of the principles involved must be questioned.**

103

salvaging it. That same party, while using the wreck for personal or professional gain, is now attempting to prevent others from doing the same. Having thoroughly explored the *Fitzgerald* wreck site, and taken everything from photographs to a rare artifact, his position now is "Let's get the media and the victims' relatives to pressure the Canadian government into declaring the wreck a gravesite, off-limits to further exploration."

Despite the obvious hypocrisy, his position still seems easily defended. Who could be in favor of photographing gravesites or strolling among the graves of the dead?

The fact is that gravesites are commonly visited by many people for many reasons. Some are drawn to pay their final respects to loved ones lost, others for different but equally valid reasons. Cemeteries are museums, filled with wonderfully creative pieces of art and architecture. History is brought to life, in oddly enough, cemeteries. Many people enjoy taking photographs and "rubbings" of headstones. Far from being considered grave desecration, it is thought to be a respectable hobby, nearly an art form.

> *Gravesites are commonly visited by many people for many reasons.*

If shipwrecks are made off-limits because they are also gravesites, then to be consistent, access to cemeteries must also be restricted. A short leap of logic could include Civil War battlefields, the final resting place for thousands, and some national parks, which host hundreds of thousands of visitors annually.

If it is one's intention to exclude only the *Fitzgerald* site from future exploration, then what characteristic singles the wreck out for that distinction?

It is certainly not the only wreck known to contain human remains. According to one well-respected researcher and author, the *Emperor*, *Kamloops*, and *Superior City* are just a few of those known to contain bodies.

> *If shipwrecks are made off-limits because they are also gravesites, then to be consistent, access to cemeteries must also be restricted.*

The *Fitzgerald* isn't even close to holding the record for greatest number of casualties, that distinction belongs to the steamer *Eastland,* which capsized at her Chicago pier July 24, 1915, taking 835 souls with her.

Examining the circumstances of the wreck, it is apparent that the only unique trait is that the "Fitz" is, to date, the longest ship to sink in the Great Lakes. While historically interesting, that would be an arbitrary reason for making the site off-limits.

Michael Neuman

An argument could be made that since human remains have been located within plain view of anyone with the technical expertise to get there, that qualifies it for special consideration. I submit that special consideration is justified whenever and wherever human remains are found.

To sensationalize the discovery of a body or the condition of a body, as was perhaps done in the case of the *Edmund Fitzgerald*, not only expresses an insensitivity to the victim's loved ones, but also demonstrates an unprofessionalism contrary to the philosophical convictions of any of the historical groups of which I am currently a member, or have ever been a member.

Designating any Great Lakes shipwreck off-limits is an immoderate measure, harming those wishing to pursue legitimate exploratory interests. The *Fitzgerald* wreck site holds significant historical interest for many, if for no other reason than it is a Great Lakes shipwreck. Over the past 150 years, thousands of ships have been wrecked in the Great Lakes, many of those taking human lives with them. All of those ships, and the men and women who died on them, have a special place in the hearts and minds of those who appreciate Great Lakes maritime history.

Whether to ban exploration on a shipwreck known to contain human remains, is a complex and controversial issue. Perhaps, when practical, an effort should be made to bring the remains to the surface for proper interment.

In the specific case of the *Edmund Fitzgerald,* according to one news source, the private

> *Whether to ban exploration on a shipwreck known to contain human remains, is a complex and controversial issue.*

companies that had provided the support ships for one of the expeditions had also volunteered their use for a recovery mission. For reasons unknown, the Canadian authorities apparently declined the offer.

Whatever is eventually decided, bear in mind that every year newer and better technology becomes available for exploring the depths. Every year more shipwrecks will be found with the potential for discovering more human remains.

A representative of the surviving families of the *Edmund Fitzgerald* tragedy was asked to contribute a response to Mr. Neuman's article but declined to do so. It is also interesting to note that during a debate of this issue in Sault Ste. Marie, Michigan, members of the Great Lakes Shipwreck Historical Society had to be removed by police because of the members' disruptive behavior.

Nick Burnett
New Diver

Nick Burnett, 14, lives in St. Ignace, Michigan. He is featured in a maritime heritage documentary produced by the Great Lakes Diving Council (GLDC). Nick has also written a book about his diving adventures; both the book and documentary are entitled *The Best Adventure Yet*. The book was published by the GLDC and is available at dive centers and bookstores throughout the Midwest.

Nick enjoys baseball, reading, walking in the woods, bike riding, and, of course, scuba diving.

Nicholas Burnett

Exploring underwater always looked exciting on television. Living at the Straits of Mackinac, which is known for its shipwrecks, made diving even more appealing. But scuba diving always seemed like a wild dream--one that would probably never become real--until I met some divers.

One of my classmates, Jason Harrington, always talked about how much fun it was to explore Great Lakes shipwrecks or tropical reefs. The more Jason talked, the more I knew I wanted to try it. But training and equipment are not easy to buy when you're 13 years old. Fortunately, Jason's father, Steve, arranged for me to obtain both so I could finally experience what I had long wanted to try--real shipwreck diving!

In class, I quickly learned how much there is to know about diving.

There is a lot more than just breathing underwater! I learned about the equipment, equalizing air pressures, nitrogen narcosis, and the dangers of going too deep. It was a lot of reading and hard studying but when it was time for open water testing, I was ready.

One of our open water dives was on a shipwreck that was broken up by waves and ice. The ship was a steamer called the *Herman H. Hettler* and had been lost in a storm off Grand Island near Munising, Mich., in 1926. Finally, I would get my chance to try shipwreck diving!

The shipwreck rested in about 25 feet of water and I was amazed not only by the size of the timbers and planks used to construct the wooden hull, but also by the number and variety of plants and animals living on or near the wreck. I swam slowly and paused often to examine crayfish and sculpins. I also had fun playing with funny green stuff I later learned was freshwater sponge.

Usually, I am the one always pushing my way to the front of the line or running ahead. But underwater I discovered a whole new world where everything seemed remarkable and new. I found an old wrench that had a layer of crust all over it. I took the time underwater to clean it off a bit and it caused me to wonder about the sailor who had touched the tool last, what happened to him, and whether other divers had seen the wrench before me and wondered the same things.

Underwater I discovered a whole new world where everything seemed remarkable and new.

Before the dive was over I had the opportunity to explore the remains of the hull in detail. I saw how large steel spikes were used to hold timbers together. I also saw how the forces of waves and ice broke the ship apart and scattered its remains on the bottom.

Newspaper accounts of the time described the *Herman H. Hettler* as a total loss. But I knew otherwise. I knew that anything that provided this much enjoyment has value. Like the divers who had gone before me, I left all of the artifacts at the site and the only souvenir I took was the memory of my first dive on a real Great Lakes shipwreck.

My first shipwreck dive didn't involve a search for gold like the dives I had seen on television. Instead, I found strange new plants and animals and wreckage from long ago. These things may not be as valuable as gold in many people's eyes, but to me they are a precious part of a whole new world I am just beginning to explore. I have discovered that each dive is a new experience and that I do not have to always dive shipwrecks or go deep to have fun. I have found fascinating plants and animals in even very shallow water and they are all part of the adventure in this world that is so new to me.

Another important part of diving is the people I dive with. My friendships with Jason and Steve have grown through diving and I have met plenty of other interesting divers, too. I've found that others enjoy the underwater world as much as I and sharing it with others is part of the fun.

My next dive? I'll be going as soon as I have the next opportunity and I'll go as often and in as many places as I can. Eventually, I may dive enough to understand this new world I've discovered. Even if I don't understand everything about it, I know I'll be having fun!

**Nick Burnett ready for his
next diving adventure!**

Ric Mixter
Videographer and
Documentary Producer

Ric Mixter is a videojournalist from Sands, Michigan. A diver since 1991, his underwater videography has included profiles of more than a dozen Great Lakes shipwrecks. His work won top honors from the Michigan Association of Broadcasters for a profile on the Thunder Bay Underwater Preserve near Alpena, Michigan. Ric also won an Associated Press award for a documentary on the Great Storm of 1913.

Ric was an underwater cameraman on submarine expeditions to the *Edmund Fitzgerald* and the *Carl D. Bradley*. Ric wrote and produced *The Best Adventure Yet*, a maritime heritage documentary, for the Great Lakes Diving Council. He lives with his wife and three children in Saginaw, Michigan.

"You should have seen this wreck in the 1960s!"

I can't tell how many times I've heard that from "pioneer" divers who braved the cold lakes before drysuits. It is amazing to think wrecks such as the *Smith Moore* or *Regina* could be any more interesting. But they certainly were for those who first saw decks filled with tools, blocks, belay pins, wheels, compasses, bells, whistles, and other brass items.

Many of these artifacts are relinquished to personal garage museums where they are slowly disintegrating. Had they been left on the bottom, these artifacts would likely be well-preserved by the cold, fresh water of the Great Lakes.

I am a news reporter and videographer with very little

> *Many of these artifacts are relinquished to personal garage museums where they are slowly disintegrating.*

training in archaeology. But I see many parallels between the two occupations.

For a news photographer, there is nothing worse than being the last person on the "scene". Details as to what happened are often confused after the story is told again and again, and clues as to what actually happened are often in the wrong place or missing altogether.

This is also true of shipwrecks. While the term "time capsules" is perhaps overused, it certainly fits. The day of the tragedy is frozen in time, not just as a memorial to what happened, but also as a window on history. And those who first peer into this window of the past have a certain responsibility, especially when they plan on documenting the site with photos or videos.

Underwater video equipment has now become affordable for most divers. And while the development of scuba equipment may be celebrating its silver anniversary, affordable, commercial underwater housings are only a decade or so old. The "Video-Age" of Great Lakes exploration is just now beginning, although it may be a bit late.

Underwater video equipment has now become affordable for most divers.

We who venture into the depths to record history carry more weight than what we wear around our waists. We also bear the burden of recording facts, which are sometimes not as exciting as the truth. All underwater video is interesting because it is a view that only a handful of people have the opportunity of viewing. But not all underwater photographers and videographers agree, as recent investigations have proven.

Some divers have moved artifacts for "better" pictures, and this includes human remains. Nothing is more sacred than a grave, and while many may argue about the ethics of obtaining images of bodies, few will approve of desecration.

Filmmakers often reconstruct scenes for dramatic effects, and reporters sometimes "stage" shots to make stories more interesting. Leave this to Hollywood and not to our one-of-a-kind shipwrecks. Moving a telegraph arm from "full ahead" erases the fact that the ship was underway when it sank. Transferring the captain's field glasses to the bridge destroys the validity of future investigations because the historical record of the vessel was altered.

Perhaps just as damaging is the "littering" of wreck sites with garbage or tag lines. It was shocking to see a photo of a diver leaving a beer can inside the pilothouse of the *Edmund Fitzgerald*. Coaxed by a family member of the crew, the team did what was "politically correct" and trashed the Great Lakes' most famous shipwreck.

Imagine what archaeologists may think when they probe the wrecksite in 50 years. They may conclude, like in the case of the *Exxon Valdez*, that alcohol may have played a role in the disaster. This legacy is fair to neither Capt. Ernest McSorley or future generations seeking to learn about our maritime heritage. Only the documentation of this event in National Geographic magazine provides hope that future researchers will realize that the beverage was not related to the tragedy.

Only divers can decide what is right. Strict laws that protect wrecks are difficult to enforce, especially when violations involve remote wreck sites.

Proper buoyancy control will keep divers from disturbing wrecks and skilled lighting and image composition will make every shot worth viewing. Learn by reviewing all footage and improve by scouting wrecks prior to filming or taping. Avoid "touring" the wreck while the camera is rolling, unless you are simply attempting to document everything there. Videotaping is an inexpensive way to record "virgin" wrecks for closer study out of the water, but that film is rarely interesting to nondivers.

Ric Mixter surfaces from a Great Lakes shipwreck dive--video recorder in tow.

Visualize shots and light them accordingly. Avoid too many special effects when it is pulled together. Nothing is more distracting than a zooming graphic superimposed over gracefully gliding divers.

Shipwrecks are interesting, regardless of condition. Each one has a unique story and it is easy to tell that story if details are recorded with cameras.

A well-produced video introduces the sport to nondivers and provides the most visual means of coaxing people to "get wet". It is new divers who must realize that we have made mistakes in the past and that they can prevent destruction of wrecks yet to be found.

Also important to keep in mind is that the maritime heritage represented by Great Lakes shipwrecks belongs to everyone-- not just divers. By sharing shipwrecks through videos and photos, divers perform a valuable public service and help others touch history so important to us all.

It is new divers who must realize that we have made mistakes in the past and that they can prevent destruction of wrecks yet to be found.

If divers feel they must move or steal artifacts to tell the story of shipwrecks, it is better that they move to Hollywood. They will make more money there.

Frank Mays
Shipwreck Survivor

On November 18, 1958, the 640-foot freighter, *Carl D. Bradley*, broke up in a storm and sank in northern Lake Michigan. Aboard the stricken ship was a 26-year-old deck watchman named Frank Mays. His inspirational story of survival and his views on visits to the shipwreck are worthy topics.

Frank was interviewed by Steve Harrington on two occasions. Here, Frank shares his thoughts and hopes for the future.

Frank Mays
Photo courtesy of
DeepQuest Publishing, Ltd.

Sinking of the *Carl D. Bradley*

On Monday, November 17, 1958, the *Carl D. Bradley* unloaded the last of her limestone cargo at Buffington, Indiana and started up Lake Michigan for its home port of Rogers City, Michigan. It was the last trip of the season for the freighter and it was scheduled to undergo major repairs before the next season.

The *Carl D. Bradley* set many shipping records since its construction in 1927 in Lorain, Ohio, and was the longest vessel on the Great Lakes at the time of her launching. In 1958, the *Carl D. Bradley* had traveled more than 27,000 miles on the Great Lakes, primarily hauling limestone to lower Lake Michigan cities for steel manufacturing.

Aboard the *Carl D. Bradley* was Frank Mays, a 26-year-old deck watchman who felt lucky to have obtained a job aboard the ship shortly after graduating from Rogers City High School. "It was considered a prime job because it paid well and because you were aboard ship, there was little place to spend money so you could easily save," he said.

Frank was not the only Rogers City native aboard. Twenty-five others also called Rogers City their home port. Of the remaining crew, only two were from out-of-state. Two were from St. Ignace. The crew quickly became a close-knit team and the building storm on

Frank was not the only Rogers City native aboard.

November 17 was of little concern, despite growing concerns about the vessel's structural integrity.

But the next day, 65 m.p.h. winds whipped up waves to as high as 30 feet. The *Carl D. Bradley* was empty but had taken on 9,000 gallons of ballast water before leaving Buffington. It appeared to be handling the rough weather well and, having made the turn near the Beaver Islands, the seas were following--generally much less dangerous.

At 5:15 p.m., Capt. Roland Bryan radioed a routine message and expected to bring the vessel to port about 2 a.m. in Rogers City the next morning. Only 16 minutes later, First Mate Elmer Fleming was screaming "May Day!" into the radio as the *Carl D. Bradley* broke in two and began a slow descent to the bottom.

In the sudden confusion, there was no time to launch life boats. When the bow of the great vessel slipped beneath them, Frank Mays and Elmer Fleming were fortunate enough to emerge near the ship's only life raft--an orange platform mounted on steel drums. As they climbed aboard in the mountainous seas, they watched tragedy unfold.

"It is something I'll never forget," Frank says. "The event is forever burned in my memory."

"The bow had already sunk and the stern section was floating when it suddenly was thrust vertically and made a slow descent to the bottom. I could

As they climbed aboard in the mountainous seas, they watched tragedy unfold.

see that the lights were still on in the stern section and suddenly there was a red ball of flame and an explosion. That was when the boilers burst," Frank says.

"Even after the explosion the stern lights were still lit but the ship continued to slowly sink and the lights disappeared one by one. It was an awesome sight."

It was a long, cold night for the two men and they were able to find two more crewmen, who joined them on the raft. Together, the four

The Carl D. Bradley--Photo courtesy Brian Bluekamp

huddled on the pitching raft. When they were pitched off by a massive wave, they helped each other back on and huddled again. On one occasion, however, one crewman did not return to the raft.

Then, at about 8:15 a.m. on November 19, another crewmen, delirious from exposure, slipped off the raft and into the dark water. Fifteen minutes later, the raft was spotted by a U.S. Coast Guard helicopter from Traverse City. Frank Mays and Elmer Fleming were the only survivors left to tell the story of the last minutes of the *Carl D. Bradley*.

Fleming died in 1977 and Frank Mays went on to work as a manufacturing representative. He is now retired and lives in Pensacola, Florida. He sometimes returns to Michigan to visit friends and relatives in Rogers City. It is a bittersweet reunion filled with the memories of the tragic losses and his fortunate escape from death on a cold November night.

It is a bittersweet reunion filled with the memories of the tragic losses and his fortunate escape from death on a cold November night.

Frank Mays--40 Years Later

Now, nearly 40 years after the disaster, Frank Mays remembers the loss of the *Carl D. Bradley* as though it had happened just a few hours ago. Time has not erased the terror-etched images of the sinking ship and the loss of his friends. But it is easier for him to talk about the disaster. Time seems to have healed his heart enough to allow him to express his feelings and memories.

"Soon after the disaster, it wasn't always easy returning to Rogers City," he said. "Among some of the crew's families, there seemed to be a feeling of unfairness that I survived when their loved ones did not. No one said anything directly to me, but it was awkward."

"Today, those feelings seem to have faded and, except for one family member, I am accepted in the community again. That is a good feeling."

> *There seemed to be a feeling of unfairness that I survived when their loved ones did not.*

Frank often pauses to select his words carefully. He wants to be accurate; to pay appropriate tribute to his lost friends, neighbors, and comrades.

"Perhaps one of the most rewarding moments I've had in returning to Rogers City was talking with the children of the men who were lost. There was one man who was an infant at the time of the disaster and never knew his father. I sat with him for hours and told him about the man. He was very appreciative, and I was, too."

Frank has discovered that many people in Rogers City carry faded photos of loved ones lost on the *Carl D. Bradley*. He still responds to questions about those last moments and the crew. Talking about these topics with family and friends seems therapeutic for Frank.

"It is still painful to remember but at least people are more willing to discuss it," Frank says. "Rogers City and the *Bradley* were so closely tied. It is just impossible to separate the two. This is a case where maritime history continues to have a profound effect on contemporary life in this community."

> *It is still painful to remember but at least people are more willing to discuss it.*

But Frank's interest in maritime history is not confined to the *Carl*

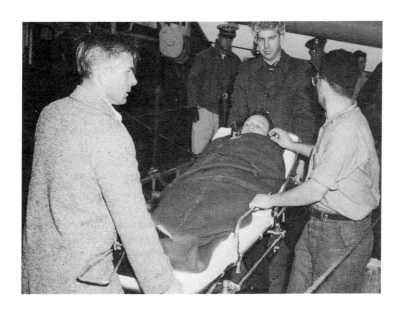

**Frank Mays was plucked from the cold Lake Michigan
water 20 miles from the wreck site.**

D. Bradley and Rogers City.

"It is interesting to see how much emphasis we place on world and national history but fail to bring it down to local communities. Here, we have an event that continues to have a profound effect on a local community and I'm not sure we really place enough attention on local maritime history. If that is true of Rogers City, it is also true for other communities," Frank said.

In August 1995, Frank joined Fred Shannon of DeepQuest, Ltd., to explore the remains of the *Carl D. Bradley*, which lie in about 350 feet of water near Beaver Island. He said the experience was remarkable.

"I thought that ship was out of my life when I saw the last lights of the stern disappear," he says. "When we dove down I was straining to see in the dark and suddenly there it was--the deck. We explored as much as we could and it sent chills through me when I saw the ship's name, as clear as though it had just been painted, on the aft section."

> *I thought that ship was out of my life when I saw the last lights of the stern disappear.*

As inspiring as the exploration was for Frank, it raised concerns among one Rogers City surviving family member about the appropriateness of visiting the wreck site.

Fueled by a telephone call from the Great Lakes Shipwreck Historical Society, she argued that the remains of the great ship are a gravesite and should not be explored. Frank disagrees.

"It is like a cemetery," he says. "We treated that site with the utmost reverence and respect. Family members do not have an exclusive market on sensitivity. These were my friends and neighbors, too. I would not participate in anything that would disrespect them."

Family members do not have an exclusive market on sensitivity.

For the most part, Frank says family members have expressed gratitude for his participation in the expedition, which saw the placement of a brass plaque containing the names of the lost crew.

"For many, this brings some solace because it is like a tombstone. It brings a sense of closure for them," he said.

What is <u>your</u> best adventure?

For 13-year-old Nick Burnett, the best adventure he could have is diving a real Great Lakes shipwreck. One summer, he discovered dreams can come true!

On his way to open water certification, Nick meets many interesting people who give him advice about diving and shipwrecks. He learns that diving is indeed a great adventure but with such adventures come certain responsibilities.

This book is written for young-adult to adult

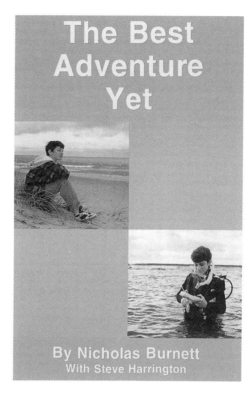

readers and features maritime archaeologists, historians, and diving pioneer Jean-Michel Cousteau.

This is a book for everyone interested in shiwprecks, maritime heritage, or diving. Written from a teen's point of view, it is a compelling story of discovery and exploration. Join Nick as he embarks on an exciting adventure!

The Best Adventure Yet is available at most book stores, dive retailers, or directly from the Great Lakes Diving Council for $6, which includes sales tax, shipping, and handling. To order your copy, send a check to:

Great Lakes Diving Council, Inc.
P.O. Box 759
St. Ignace, MI 49781

New Edition!

Divers Guide to Michigan

The most popular guide to diving in Michigan just got better! It has been revised and expanded to include more dive sites, more shipwrecks, and more information!

The new edition also contains more maps, drawings of shipwrecks, and photographs. The guide also includes information about the state's two newest underwater preserves--DeTour Passage and the Southwest Michigan Underwater Preserves.

This handy guide has become a trusty companion for many Great Lakes divers because it provides information about the history of shipwrecks, how to find dive sites, emergency procedures, support services such as charters and air stations, lodging, and other information to make diving more enjoyable.

The pages are packed with practical tips and easy directions to find the best diving in Michigan. Look for **Divers Guide to Michigan** at your local bookstore or dive retailer.

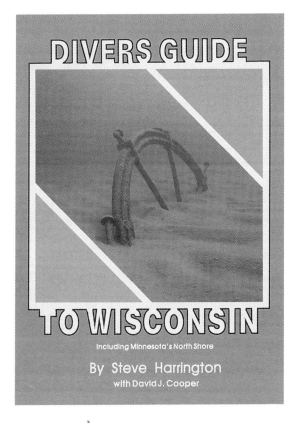

DIVERS GUIDE TO WISCONSIN

Including Minnesota's North Shore

By Steve Harrington
with David J. Cooper

Divers Guide to Wisconsin

This is the complete guide to diving in Wisconsin waters!

This guide covers Wisconsin diving in Lake Michigan and Lake Superior and also many of the great inland dive sites.

In addition to diving tips, **Divers Guide to Wisconsin** provides maps, a brief history of shipwrecks, and emergency procedures. Divers will also enjoy quick reference to dive-support services such as air stations and charters as well as information about lodging and family attractions.

The guide is packed with maps, coordinates, tips, photographs, and drawings. It even includes a summary of state laws, maritime history, and a glossary of shipwreck terms.

Special chapters cover Door County, the Apostle Islands, inland dive sites, and shipwrecks along the Lake Michigan coast.

This book has quickly become the standard for Wisconsin divers. **Divers Guide to Wisconsin** can be found at most book stores and dive retailers. Get your copy today and find what you've been missing!

Great Lakes Diving Council

A private, nonprofit organization

The Great Lakes Diving Council (GLDC), Inc., is a private, nonprofit organization dedicated to diver education and the promotion of diving of all sorts in the Great Lakes region. The GLDC has undertaken several important initiatives, including the publication and distribution of a boating and diving poster and a comprehensive maritime heritage education program.

In addition, the GLDC is working with other organizations to facilitate key projects that will enhance sport diving. A good example is the intentional vessel sinking project at the Alger Underwater Preserve.

The GLDC also monitors important state and federal legislation that could affect sport diving. Members receive a quarterly newsletter that details diving developments throughout the Great Lakes. Business members receive marketing assistance and special publications.

If you want to keep abreast of sport diving developments in the Great Lakes region, join us! Membership fees support publication of the newsletter and educational projects of the GLDC. Annual membership dues are $10 for individuals and $25 for businesses and other organizations.

To join the GLDC, send a check to:

Great Lakes Diving Council, Inc.
P.O. Box 759
St. Ignace, MI 49781